YOUR OPPORTUNITY RIVER

YOUR OPPORTUNITY RIVER

INCREASE THE FLOW OF PROFITS
AND SCALE YOUR MANUFACTURING ORGANIZATION

GREG LAKE

LIONCREST
PUBLISHING

YOUR OPPORTUNITY RIVER
Increase the Flow of Profits and Scale Your Manufacturing Organization

FIRST EDITION

ISBN   978-1-5445-4535-6   *Hardcover*
        978-1-5445-4534-9   *Paperback*
        978-1-5445-4533-2   *Ebook*

To everyone in the manufacturing industry. You are the makers of the things we all enjoy in this world. I am proud to be a part of your industry.

CONTENTS

INTRODUCTION 9

1. BUSINESS LESSONS FROM A RIVER............................ 17

2. MAP YOUR OPPORTUNITY RIVER 33

3. IT'S ALL ABOUT THE FLOW................................. 45

4. SEEKING OUT OBSTRUCTIONS............................... 59

5. STRAIGHTEN YOUR OPPORTUNITY RIVER.................... 75

6. OPEN THE FLOOD GATES................................... 85

7. MAKE YOUR OPPORTUNITY RIVER FOREVER GREEN 95

8. CREATING FLOW MONITORS 105

9. RIVER OF DREAMS 119

10. TWO VIEWS OF YOUR OPPORTUNITY RIVER 131

CONCLUSION 143

ACKNOWLEDGMENTS 145

INTRODUCTION

IMAGINE THE FOLLOWING SITUATION—OR MAYBE you don't have to imagine if you are currently experiencing something similar. As the chief operating officer (COO) of ABC Fabrications, Frank was at the center of every aspect of internal operations in his four-hundred-plus person manufacturing organization. ABC Fab specialized in metal fabrication for various industries. It was Frank's job to grow the company by leveraging their decades of experience, maximizing the potential of the office and shop floor, assisting sales in taking on big new customers, and communicating expectations clearly with every level of management. He also had to keep the bankers informed and happy, because they funded the company's growth to effectively serve hundreds of customers across the Midwest.

His responsibilities were significant, his ambitions were high, yet a few hurdles were standing in Frank's way. To begin with, ABC Fab was maxed out. The economy was hot, and ABC Fab was running at record revenue. But there was no available capacity. In addition, customers were complaining about delays, and orders were coming in so fast that accurate delivery dates were impossible to determine. The biggest hurdle for Frank, though, was eroding profitability. True to form, ABC Fab grew revenue from the prior year by roughly 7 percent, or $9 million, but with profit growth of only $100,000, or 1.1 percent.

How could Frank take on new business when the profits were so meager? Work-in-process (WIP) and raw material inventory were piling up. Cash was going out faster than it was coming in, consuming lines of credit. Every day was a firefight, with fires erupting throughout the organization.

Production couldn't produce fast enough.

What would you do? Throw money at the problems? That's what most manufacturers would do. They would get more resources by hiring more people, adding more inventory, buying more machines, and adding more facilities. That is the norm in the industry. Unfortunately, the outcome of such efforts is usually increased overhead, a higher breakeven point, and tied up available credit—all of which put added risk on the company when/if the economy ultimately cools down.

I would like to offer a better solution. In this book, I will show you how using the metaphor of a river can create valuable strategies that transform how you view, run, and scale your manufacturing organization—all while addressing the inefficiencies and disruptions that are lowering your profitability. No matter how small or large your manufacturing company, you can transform it to be more resilient, more efficient, and more profitable. At the same time, it will weather the ups and downs of the economy and run with incredible clarity through every aspect of the internal processes. And to make it your own, we will call it Your Opportunity River.

YOUR RIVER AWAITS

Before I started The Lake Companies, Inc. in 1983, I worked in the planning department for a manufacturer who made thousand-foot Great Lakes ore carriers. It was easy to sense the frustration running throughout the company. There were enormous problems in how the company operated, but somehow, it was never the right time to do anything about them. We were either in the position of being too busy or not busy enough to fix most issues standing in our way. And the gap between those two positions seemed to get smaller and smaller every year. For this reason, when we did address issues, it was often too late and always too expensive. Today, forty years later, the exact same thing is still happening across the manufacturing industry. Companies are either too busy or not busy enough to fix problems, even when the problems are stifling their growth and profitability. And when they do fix those problems, it's always expensive.

There is a fatalism in manufacturing, one built on the assumption that the only way to address many internal operations issues is by throwing money at them. This is due to an inability to know how to truly tackle issues that are hiding in plain sight. Where do you start? And if making changes—rocking the boat—only leads to more chaos, why start at all? Little ever changes in the shuffle from feast to famine…or flood to drought.

Today is the day to chart a more profitable course. As the late entrepreneur Jim Rohn said, "If you really want to do something, you'll find a way." This is the way.

Your Opportunity River can solve the complexities in your business without throwing your company into chaos. Finding the challenges in your company isn't an unsolvable puzzle. In fact, I saw this work firsthand all the way back in 1992. The CEO of one of The Lake Companies' customers clued me in to how he generated an almost unheard-of boon in his business. For the first time, they finished the year dramatically growing revenue *and* profits at the same time. Before that, it had always been a trade-off between the two.

Okay, the company did purchase our ERP software and yes, it did have an impact. But I don't believe the benefits were all a result of the software. There are far too many companies who have reliable ERP systems that struggle with the exact same problems. ERP can help create that boon, but it won't be the sole force. That has to come from changes to the company's internal operations.

As I realized this, I began to study more closely the inner workings of other organizations inside and outside manufacturing to see how improving flow allowed them to grow more effectively. The result was Your Opportunity River.

WHO SHOULD READ THIS BOOK

We have all experienced a rain shower that started out being exactly what your yard needed only to expand into an overwhelming storm. Suddenly, the gentle shower increased intensity, the wind started blowing, and the sky seemingly opened up into a raging downpour. In a short time, the local creeks and rivers started to flood, creating destruction everywhere.

And I bet you have experienced your company when new orders were coming in faster than anyone could imagine and with little advance notice; it felt like you were hit with a tidal wave. Everywhere you looked, people were struggling to keep their heads above water. Challenges were coming from every angle, just like being hit with a wall of water. Business as usual just ended, and all you could do was deal with the pandemonium to survive.

If you have experienced those situations, this book is for you. I am speaking to you if you own or work for a manufacturer, particularly one who produces products in industries like metal fabrication, industrial machinery & equipment, contract machining, aerospace & defense, high-tech & electronics, medical devices, furniture & fixtures, specialty vehicles, RVs & transportation equipment, window & door, as well as general discrete manufacturing.

More specifically, if you experience the roller-coaster swings in business from feast to famine—from flood to drought, from monsoon rains to desert dryness—and do not have a solution to the varying levels of business other than to just increase or decrease your internal resources (people, inventory, machinery, and facilities), then this book is for you. If your organization has gone through endless searching without a way to find enough good people, please keep reading. I have a solution you should be interested in.

MY PROMISE TO YOU

By the end of this book, you will have a map of Your Opportunity River and a clear understanding of how to increase profitability and capacity, allowing your company to grow revenue, even when facing a "when it rains, it pours" storm of orders. At the same time, you will find out how to lower your breakeven level and fuel record profits. Best of all, you will know how to accomplish this by harvesting significant value from your internal resources before investing a single additional dime in any one of them.

That's certainly the experience Frank had. Using these ideas, he transformed ABC Fab into a huge success story, with profits outpacing stellar revenue growth.

Don't delay. The economy changes quickly, and a sudden

downswing can have a devastating impact on any business, while a sudden upswing can create new levels of chaos. So, let's get started on helping you harvest significant value from your business immediately.

So many books I've read over the years were long, and after the first half of the book, they dried up with little more to share. That will not be the case here. I've kept this book short, with nonstop benefits from cover to cover. Each chapter provides secrets that will help you get control and stay in control of your organization's future. In fact, each new chapter's secrets will accelerate the value, all the way to the end.

Let's dive right in.

SCAN HERE

Scan now for a quick video summary of this chapter!

Dive into key insights in seconds.

https://qrco.de/yor08kpt

CHAPTER 1

BUSINESS LESSONS FROM A RIVER

FRANK, WHOM WE MET IN THE INTRODUCTION, faced some formidable problems if he wanted to transform ABC Fab into a fast-growing, high-profit, well-organized manufacturing operation. To begin with, the company had major cash flow problems. Inventory was often purchased at great expense months before an order entered production, only to be warehoused and sometimes misplaced before the shop floor was ready to work with it. The cash for these projects took even longer to come in, with the gap between cash going out and cash coming in exceeding production time by many months. This created shortfalls that could only be financed through bank loans. And the bank, in turn, put restrictions on the company's lines of credit, reducing Frank's ability to invest when there was an opportunity to increase sales.

That wasn't all. Costs for the production of each project were impossible to manage in real time because there was no way to review the process or costs until the order was completed. Once an order was placed in the queue for production, the best anyone could do was manage by walking around (MBWA). It didn't help that the company's supposedly state-of-the-art computer system crashed multiple times a day, reducing Frank's ability to track orders even further.

With each of these issues, profitability was lost, growth was slowed, and disorder crept into production. With slim margins and large loans, the company was exposed to significant risk. The COVID-19 pandemic and the tight labor market afterward had taught Frank that a future supply chain disruption, any more tightening of an already limited supply of labor, or a sudden dip in the economy could leave ABC Fab in a desperate situation.

For that reason, each of these issues was a major problem, but it wasn't *the* problem at ABC Fab. Frank couldn't solve any of these issues because he couldn't *see* what was causing them. They were all so complex and so well hidden in the workings of the internal operations of the company that most assumed this was just the cost of doing business.

If Frank was going to change anything, he'd have to find a new way to conceive of ABC's internal operations. Otherwise, he'd be up the creek without a paddle.

A SIMPLER VIEW

Located 646 miles from the Gateway Arch in St. Louis, Missouri, and 182 miles northwest of St. Anthony's Falls in Minneapolis-St. Paul, lies a small and seemingly insignificant lake embedded in the deciduous forest of north central Minnesota. Unlike the hundreds of other lakes that populate this area, Lake Itasca is conspicuous from all the other lakes in that it serves as the birthplace of the mighty Mississippi River.

From high above looking down at the north side of this lake, a small, inconsequential stream of water can be seen escaping over a small confluence of stones at the lake's edge, creating a winding creek that in some places appears as though one could easily jump across it.

Once the water reaches Little Falls, Minnesota, and the stream matures to constitute a true river, it begins to chart a definitive course as it swells to ever greater depth and size.

The Mississippi River serves as an enormous drainage basin to more than one-third of the United States and parts of Canada for a total area of 1.2 million to 1.8 million square miles, and it hosts tributary rivers such as the St. Croix, the Wisconsin, the Illinois, the Ohio, the Arkansas, and the great Missouri. The Mississippi River eventually channels over three million cubic feet of water per second.

Wait. Why am I talking about rivers? The facts above may be interesting, but what do they have to do with Frank? And what do they have to do with you and your manufacturing company? Interestingly enough, everything.

The Mississippi River provides an excellent example of not just how a river grows but how a manufacturing company grows—and overcomes its current inefficiencies, revenue limits, and constrained profits. The river metaphor, or what I call Your Opportunity River, makes the manufacturing process—its strengths, its goals, and its obstacles—understandable so everyone can bring thoughts and ideas to the table to make significant growth possible.

This simpler view starts with swapping the water in a river with the revenue in a manufacturing company. In a river, water runs from the start of the river to its end, with the water eventually flowing to another tributary, a lake, sea, or ocean. In a manufacturing company, every sales order can be thought of as revenue flowing from the start of the river (taking an order) to its end (shipping and invoicing the product). Consistent product orders can fill the river with revenue that flows through the company and down the river, resulting in shipments to customers, invoicing, and collecting cash at the end.

All along a river in nature are its riverbanks, some low and some high. If the volume of water flowing down the river is great enough, flooding will happen everywhere the banks are not high enough to contain the flow. It is typically pretty easy to see where flooding can happen along a river, just by seeing the height of its banks. Yet a major storm can create surprise flooding, even in areas where the banks seem high. Flooding, as you know, happens when the volume of water in the river exceeds its capacity. Increasing the capacity of any stretch of the river is typically done by raising the bank where flooding typically occurs.

Let's compare that to a manufacturer. Most manufacturers have a reasonable understanding of their shop floor capacity, and they routinely increase the capacity by adding overtime, more people, shifts, equipment, and/or facilities. On the shop floor, capacity problems are fairly obvious when orders start flooding in. WIP inventory from resulting jobs stops flowing and backs up around the areas that lack capacity. While it is relatively easy to spot flow problems on the shop floor, on Your Opportunity River, much of the length of the river flows through the back office to get to the shop floor— which is where a surprising amount of flooding takes place.

Do you know the capacity of order processing, planning, purchasing, accounting, or even inventory control? In the office, there are no banks to be seen. There are no metrics that show capacity. How high are the related banks and when do they become the source of flooding? And what does flooding mean in such areas?

Quite simply, when the volume of revenue flowing through any department exceeds its banks, the resulting flood means revenue is flowing over the riverbanks of that department, creating some level of destruction to the profitability of the company.

On the other hand, drought can happen in a river with the lack of precipitation to the point where the river bottom is exposed, and the flow can come to a complete stop, starving the areas downstream of needed water. As with a river in nature, drought starves the areas downstream, including your manufacturing process, from getting needed work. When droughts are bad enough, the lack of revenue in a down market can expose the organization's river bottom, more commonly referred to a breakeven, where the company experiences losses due to the lack of revenue.

The obvious solution to the problems of flood stage and drought are to build the banks higher throughout the organization, while at the same time lowering the river bottom to allow a wider range of revenue and greater profits. These are the solutions that will be exposed in Your Opportunity River. Whether you are a start-up manufacturer, midsized with a few hundred employees, or a giant global provider of products and services, the Opportunity River analogy can easily guide your business through the pitfalls of modern manufacturing—the lack of clarity, the endless obstacles, and the struggle for growth.

Rivers offer manufacturing leaders like you and Frank—as well as your teams—a way to visualize and conceptualize the internal operational issues holding your company back.

The problem Frank had at ABC Fab was that he couldn't keep all the vast and complex information about his internal business operations in his head at once. And when he wanted to implement changes, it was hard to explain them in a way that everyone on the team could understand, without the constant excuses as to why the changes would not work.

By mapping ABC Fab's Opportunity River, we will change that. It will create a visual metaphor to simplify every element of their operations.

Using the idea of the river, we can measure the elements of success and where attention is needed by monitoring the flow of your company's Opportunity River. As we progress, you will get a clear visual picture of how the company is performing and where it is falling short.

Instead of firefighting endless disruptions caused by missed delivery dates and angry customers, leaders like Frank can use the concepts in this book to proactively locate and remove obstacles hiding throughout the fulfillment process. Those obstacles can exist anywhere along the journey to the customer, from taking an order from a customer through to the time when products are shipped. Through the lens of Your Opportunity River, ABC Fab's product lines are viewed as a series of tributaries converging into its main river system. They become a map bringing clarity to Frank and others at ABC Fab about the interdependence these tributaries share, the nature of their relationship, and their impact on revenue and profitability.

The river metaphor is not only very precise and visual but also incredibly adaptable to the circumstances of your company. Like manufacturers, rivers come in markedly different sizes. Your manufacturing business might be enormous, like the Mississippi, medium-sized like the Ohio, or small like the Iowa, or the GOAT (Greatest of All Time), the Amazon.

Some manufacturers have hundreds of revenue streams, just as many rivers have an enormous number of tributaries. Others have only a few. Rivers, like manufacturers, are constantly facing shifts in the weather. Manufacturers face recessions and surplus demand; rivers face droughts and floods. Rivers have bends that slow how quickly the water reaches its destination; manufacturers face obstacles that impact production and delay delivery to customers.

For each river, as with each manufacturer, these elements are unique, and always present. However, when you change your mindset from the confusion of endless conflicting operational spreadsheets, reports, finger-pointing, frustrations, and helplessness, to a river of opportunities—a whole new world of possibilities can open up.

A METAPHOR FOR EVERY MANUFACTURER

John L. McCaffrey—former president of International Harvester Company when it was the world's largest manufacturer of agricultural equipment in the world—once said, "The mechanics of running a business are really not complicated when you get down to the essentials. You have to make some stuff and sell it for more than it cost you. That's about all there is to it, except for a few million details."

The question is how do you visualize those few million details? This was Frank's problem. ABC Fab made literally thousands of products, many of which were custom. They made everything from custom-cut steel parts to heavy weldments and a line of security enclosures. Some projects were massive; other projects required little more than laser cutting, surface preparation, and powder coating. All of this took place under one roof and at one time.

Managing back office operations and production should not be chaotic at the best of times, but Frank rarely saw the best of times at ABC Fab. If one thing went wrong—whether it was one of countless interruptions, including customers changing order details, a delay in materials arriving, or even a mistake on the floor—it could cascade into a series of issues across the organization. There was never a simple answer dealing with mistakes, changes, or inefficiencies.

This isn't just the case for metal fabrication companies. The issues are indiscriminate and impact every kind of manufacturer.

In each situation, the problem executives face relates to the complexities of modern manufacturing. Those complexities cause companies to fall victim to being reactive without clarity to the underlying issues and are only resolved by throwing money at more internal resources.

That's where Your Opportunity River fits in. It allows you to assimilate data to a location on a map that everyone can understand intuitively in a moment. Knowing where to look allows you to be precise in locating problems and communicating adjustments. As with problems, growth opportunities become just as easy to illustrate, often by simply drawing in a new tributary.

When your business is a river you've drawn on a napkin, a piece of paper, or a computer screen, you can make it any size you want. You can easily share it and use it to illustrate how your business is running, so you and others can easily understand what adjustments are necessary and make them efficiently. You can mark an obstacle, tackle it, and remove it. You can chart a new path, plan for it, and implement it.

Growth, profitability, and efficiency become so much easier to grasp and address.

A RIVER'S GREAT VULNERABILITIES

Along with improving your insight into your operations, the river also clarifies the forces most affecting your company—the ones that cost you profits and put your entire operation at risk. In particular, the river allows you to more clearly conceptualize the threats of floods and droughts.

PROFITS SPILLING OVER THE BANKS

A rising river can create huge problems when you live next to it. Cities and towns next to rivers are built for such occurrences, yet flooding can still happen. Those communities construct riverbanks high enough to avoid any problems during the wet season. As mentioned earlier, in manufacturing, the back office embankments are not visible, yet they represent your organizational capacity—and their banks are usually precariously low because managers don't know where the obstructions are. And because they don't know where the obstructions are, they don't really know where they're going to hit flood stage until it happens.

As a result, flood stage isn't a rare event but a constant threat, like the flooding of a river, where water spills over the banks and goes everywhere but the intended journey down the river, destroying everything in its way. Any time there is a high level of orders coming into the company, those orders that provide you with revenue result in profits that are lost through no fault of anyone in the organization.

Flood stage is the point where the company just becomes overwhelmed. There are so many orders, they can't be completed efficiently. Costs run high, everyone is working overtime, new hires are urgently needed, and profits drain away. When Frank was congratulated for generating 1.1 percent profit on $9 million in revenue, the numbers were so low because the company was in flood stage. The expectations for profits were so low because *the company was always in flood stage*.

The impact of flooding on the organization can be so subtle. Like a river, flooding can happen across the entire process or in one (or a few) locations. You may max out capacity at one or more areas of your internal operations—or in all of them, from start to finish.

Because of flooding, strong economies are often seen as a crisis. Manufacturers often find it impossible to keep up with fulfillment as the orders pour in. Because their internal operations are full of obstacles, they quickly become stressed to their limits, resulting in a logistic nightmare, with no chance to meet customer needs.

Since most manufacturers have a habit of never saying no to an order, and since they don't know where their obstructions are, they very quickly run up costs and experience delays. This puts everyone in the organization under immense pressure, strains bank credit, and often requires drastic, expensive measures to speed the process up—all of which drain all the potential profits when revenue is really raining in.

With a record backlog, a manufacturer is often forced, ironically, to increase their overhead dramatically. As they try to raise their riverbanks across the whole operation or in specific areas, they are challenged to stay ahead of the rising level of orders. In Frank's situation, during the prior year, he added more machinery, equipment, and people to take on perceived growth. If the growth came as $9 million in additional revenue, the overhead increase via the added resources ate the profits away. Unfortunately, no one has a crystal ball and can accurately predict whether the growth ABC Fab was expecting is just around the corner. Companies get put into such situations where a booming market quickly turns to bust, and the overhead further cripples the organization with more costs to cover before making a profit.

Flooding creates so much confusion and can consume so much mindshare, people, resources, and cash, it becomes a serious struggle to pool enough attention at the executive level to try to make adjustments to lessen the flooding. There's typically only one option. Throw money at the problem, with—you guessed it—more people, more inventory, more machinery, and more facilities.

In the end, any level of revenue that exceeds flood stage translates into strained operations and missed opportunities for manufacturers. Companies waste time debating which work gets priority and which will suffer additional delays. The delays result in further waste as customers complain, causing continuous priority changes. The desperate hope for the manufacturer is that most customers will simply shrug these delays off and accept that this is just how manufacturing works. But there's no guarantee they won't switch to an alternative when the market hits a rough period, sending the manufacturer into drought.

DRIED-UP DESPERATION

Flooding can be chaotic, but drought is far riskier for manufacturers. The desire to take every single order comes from a fear of drought—when orders dry up. A slow economy is bad for every business, but it can be harder on manufacturers. As we just saw, in expanding economies, manufacturers can repeatedly hit flood stage, with the need to raise their riverbanks to take on more orders—which leads to significant investment across the organization in an effort to force faster flow.

Droughts that follow market corrections are particularly precarious because manufacturers bring those heavier financial obligations into those slow periods. This means that breakeven revenues have increased as well, removing the ability to downshift as effectively as other industries. When business slows, there are still debts on those machines, leases on those facilities, and wages to pay. It isn't easy to cut those costs when machines are idle and warehouses are empty.

With little business and no easy ways to cut costs, or hold onto cash reserves, it's hardly surprising each drought claims so many manufacturers.

THREE FOCUSES OF YOUR OPPORTUNITY RIVER

As mentioned, the main thing Frank needed above all else was clarity in the internal operations of ABC Fab. Clarity would make it easier to see where the banks were lowest and where his river bottom could be deeper. To achieve that, he would need to map his river—or what was in reality, a river system.

That's the first major focus of this book. First, you gain new clarity into your business operations by mapping your river and discovering the extent of your Opportunity River system. Once you achieve that, you can move forward with the second focus: charting the obstacles that restrict the flow of your river, and targeting and removing those obstacles to create raging revenue streams in every river and tributary.

But we won't stop there—because you, like Frank, are ambitious enough to want more than just better flow. You want to grow Your Opportunity River to be as vast as the Mississippi. That's where we'll head in our last section: into a world of sustainable growth that takes you to the head of your industry and keeps you there.

With clarity, flow, and growth, your company can transform into a river system full of opportunity. And it all starts with a pencil and paper, as you, like Frank, draw out the Opportunity River map for your entire organization.

Scan now for a quick video summary of this chapter!

Dive into key insights in seconds.

https://qrco.de/yor1w13f

CHAPTER 2

MAP YOUR OPPORTUNITY RIVER

of Your Opportunity River, he asked me whether I'd been drawn to the river metaphor because of my last name, Lake. I had to admit there was something to that. I love the water and live on the water. My wife and I have more than a few sweatshirts, hats, T-shirts, drink glasses, pictures, and wall art with lake-related phrases around the house.

Considering my enthusiasm for bodies of water, it's hardly surprising I'd seize on something I noticed when looking at maps of the United States. Glancing over various mountain ranges and plains, I noticed, as if for the first time, the incredible vastness of the Mississippi River. When you really look at it, the Mississippi is such a massive and efficient waterway. It's truly an elegant work of nature.

The Mississippi River's historical role in shipping and manufacturing got me thinking about the manufacturers I worked with. If only the executives at those companies could see their operations as clearly as I could see the Mississippi laid out on my map—if only they could map their own internal operations the same way we map the Mississippi—perhaps they could see how to make their profits flow more efficiently, like the water in that mighty river system.

SEEING YOUR SURROUNDINGS

Imagine yourself on a raft floating down a revenue stream in your company. The river has signs on the banks indicating the operational areas it will flow through before it gets to manufacturing, like sales, engineering, planning, purchasing, inventory control, etc. The river is long because the product is large, complex, and takes considerable time to design and build. The raft you are riding in is one of many rafts flowing downstream. Each raft has a label on it indicating the product(s) being built, the customer who ordered them, the quantity ordered, the delivery date, etc. The label has other information the department it is flowing through will need to do their functions to process the order. The raft is supported by the money that is flowing downstream, representing the revenue for the product.

Almost immediately, you notice the money and related rafts are flowing at different speeds. Some are moving very fast, while others are moving slowly and lining up one after another. Those moving slowly seem like they are on a lazy river at a water park. Some of the rafts float around in a single department for days or even weeks before proceeding downstream to the next department. This happens from one department to the next, until the raft finally makes it though manufacturing, shipping, and invoicing, where the real money for the products will be earned and collected.

You expect the raft trip to be like a white-water rafting outing, with the river flowing like a torrent the entire journey. To your dismay, the ride is nothing like that at all. You go from one obstacle to another, each causing the river to flow at its own pace. There are areas where your raft just stops for a seemingly endless amount of time. You look at the changing days on the calendar as the raft meanders helplessly down the river. It's consuming all the lead time (the time from order to shipping), and you wonder how the product will be delivered on time. Further down the river, some of the people in the department you drift through are making jokes about another order that will not get to the customer on time.

Nobody seems to wonder whether the sale will result in a profit or not. Each department just wants to do what they can to process their share of the order and get it moving farther downstream.

Throughout the journey, you only see where you are. It's not always possible to see the next department downstream because the river is not straight. It has corners and bends, places that appear to have huge lakes. You see areas where the banks are very high and other places where the banks are precariously low, even to the point where you see money leaving the river where the river is higher than the banks. In those areas, the money is flowing everywhere but downstream. It makes you feel sick and helpless to see what is happening on your journey. But there is only so much you can do when you can't see the problems.

This isn't just a metaphor. At this moment, you're running your manufacturing business on a river without the clarity necessary to deliver your products as quickly and profitably as possible. This is happening because there is no map of your internal operations. It isn't just you. You also have twenty-five, fifty, hundreds, or perhaps thousands of people employed at your company, and none of them have a cohesive map. Just like you, they can only see a small area of operations. In too many situations, your people know their job but do not know their work's impact on others who are working upstream or downstream. Without knowing it, they could very well be hurting your operations instead of helping them.

Now is the time to change that. And we will do it by using the same technology that made it possible to navigate rivers like the Mississippi: a map.

GET READY TO DRAW YOUR OPPORTUNITY RIVER MAP

As we prepare to sketch out your company, let me reassure you that drawing Your Opportunity River map requires absolutely no artistic skill. Whether you draw like Rembrandt or a five-year-old, it's all the same. The only thing that matters is that the river reasonably reflects your reality. All you need to start is a few pieces of paper. You can also do this on a tablet, but if you do, be sure to save your work.

As you prepare to draw, be conscious that you need to leave room for adjustments. You're going to enhance elements of this river system multiple times in this book. Those adjustments are key to the value of this process. The more you adjust, the greater clarity you will be getting into how your river flows and the impact obstacles have on the flow of your river.

To guide you, I'll break down the mapping process into the essential components for this initial exercise.

THE TWO COMPONENTS OF YOUR RIVER

At this point, there are only two major elements you need to understand to draw your river. While Your Opportunity River will gain more detail as we move forward, these remain the most essential, core pieces to your river.

YOUR RIVER

As mentioned earlier, a river represents your company's entire revenue stream that flows from taking an order for your products and/or services, through production, to shipping the product to your customer.

It is important to remember that the water in the river is really the flow of money. As we progress through this book, you will identify areas where the flow of revenue is very slow, which is considered lazy cash. Other areas of the river will flow straight and fast, which is fast-moving, hard-working cash.

TRIBUTARIES

A river is only as large as the number of tributaries that feed it. A tributary is an individual revenue stream that feeds into your river. It's an individual product line or service that provides a source of income.

The way to start is to list the product lines and/or services the company sells. Any product line is typically a group of similar products. Group together those products that will take the same route through your internal operations and the shop. For instance, if you make pumping systems that move wastewater and others that move fresh water, each has similarities, yet are manufactured differently due to the nature of the material they move. They also can be sold to different customer segments. For those reasons, it would be good to separate them into different revenue streams.

Similarly, in steel parts as compared to fabricated steel weldments, the cut steel parts can go from laser cutting, to optionally bending on a press, to prep and paint, whereas the weldments require multiple parts to be cut and tack welded, prior to finish welding, followed by drilling, tapping, and prep and paint. Since the processes are so different, I would suggest different tributaries.

In many cases, companies have these product lines broken out already. Most often, they are how accounting handles the sale of the products for financial statement purposes. This method aligns very well with the individual tributary methodology.

The length of any tributary represents the lead time normally calculated in days to take an order, procure materials, schedule production, manufacture the goods, and deliver the order to the customer. Some tributaries have long lead times, and this should be designated by the length of the tributary relative to that of tributaries for other products or services in your company.

You can think of the lead time for a product or service as the number of days it would take for the raft to flow downstream, from taking an order at the beginning of the tributary to when it empties into your main river upon shipment to the customer.

Individual tributaries should be short, medium, or long to represent your average lead time. There's no need to be exact here, but as you add more tributaries, make sure the lengths of each are relative to the timeframe of order-to-invoicing.

Each tributary can have additional tributaries that flow into it. If a tributary represents a major product line, it may have many smaller tributaries for individual product and service offerings. Connect those products and services directly to the main tributary they flow through. My suggestion is to keep this at a high level at this point in time. You can always go deeper as you understand the process better.

DRAWING YOUR RIVER

To begin drawing your river, start with a simple, horizontal line across the page. This is the river into which your major tributaries will flow. Everything ultimately intersects with this one line, meaning every sale from each tributary empties into your main river, delivering revenue to your company. Next, let's add tributaries.

For simplicity's sake, let's start by drawing your largest revenue stream or product line as your main tributary. For Frank and ABC Fab, recall their product lines were cut parts of various shapes, complex weldments, and a line of security enclosures. The largest revenue stream for ABC was their security enclosures. Despite higher order volumes for the other revenue streams, especially the custom cut parts, fewer security enclosures are sold, but at much greater prices. As a result, the enclosures represent the largest revenue stream feeding into ABC's Opportunity River.

ABC's enclosure division had been a bedrock product line for decades. Because these enclosures had a long order-to-invoice lead time, Frank would draw a long tributary line that intersected with his river.

After drawing his largest tributary, Frank gave it a name (Security Enclosures). Additionally, he noted the most recent monthly revenue, profit, and profit percentage at the end of the river.

What if your company has a product line with a number of options? Or what if you build a machine that has optional accessories, like material loaders/infeed mechanisms, palletizers, conveyor systems, etc.? You would show the accessories as one or more tributaries feeding into the machine tributary the accessories are made for.

For Frank, there were several major product accessories associated with security enclosures. He represented each with its own tributary on his map flowing into the Security Enclosure tributary just mentioned.

At this point, you can begin adding more revenue streams (tributaries) that feed into your main river. Start with your next highest revenue-producing product or product line, and draw it either short, intermediate, or long depending on the average lead time. Then, just like your largest revenue stream, give them a name, along with indicating the most recent monthly revenue, profit, and profit percent for each tributary.

For ABC Fab, beyond their main tributary of security enclo-sures, they manufactured two kinds of complex weldments. The first was structural weldments built to the specifications of the customer. The second type of complex weldments was used as the foundation for a customer's industrial machinery. These foundations were highly engineered, very precise, and machined to tight tolerances.

Despite the fact that they were both weldments, the structural weldments and machine foundations were considered individual tributaries due to the additional machining process and higher costs for the foundations. Finally, since cut parts were sold to a variety of customers, they were considered a separate tributary. Even though cut parts were also used as components in both complex weldments and security enclosures, Frank drew them as a separate tributary when they were sold on their own.

This distinction is important to keep in mind. For ABC Fab's river model, cut parts, complex weldments, and security enclosures are separate tributaries *only* when they are *sold* to customers. Remember, the river deals with your revenue. It's about the product you sell, not the components used to make the product.

When you draw your tributaries, don't be concerned whether any will continue to provide the same revenue in the future. Rivers change all the time. A map is meant to show us what the river looks like *right now*. At this moment, each tributary represents a unique revenue contributor to your company.

As you review ABC Fab's river system from the illustrations, note how easy it is to understand compared to an income statement. Your Opportunity River map shows you all the major revenue generators in the company. You can also easily see which product lines have the longest lead times, which provide the most revenue, and which generate the greatest profit margins.

It's all so much clearer than a spreadsheet—and we only just got started.

SEEING THE SYSTEM BEYOND THE RIVER

With this map drawn, you can already begin to discover new insights into your company. For instance, your map makes it clear how much potential flows through your river system and its tributaries. Your company may be vast and complex, but on a single sheet of paper, you have diagrammed all the main sources of revenue, the length of lead time, and the breakdown of that revenue in one place.

But that's really just the beginning. Now it is time to use Your Opportunity River map to really get clarity on the dynamics of your river, allowing you to seek out the potential hiding places of the obstacles and challenges you face on a daily basis.

Scan now for a quick video summary of this chapter!

Dive into key insights in seconds.

https://qrco.de/yor2rw6f

CHAPTER 3

IT'S ALL ABOUT THE FLOW

LIKE OTHERS IN THE INDUSTRY, FRANK'S BIGGEST problems did not happen because of manufacturing. They just happened to get noticed in inventory and on the shop floor. You might wonder why that happens. The answer is simple. Those areas are where people can see the issues. In other words, that is where they become visual.

One of the underlying principles of Your Opportunity River is to bring out the issues in a visual way. Too often, staring at spreadsheet after spreadsheet of data only suggests a problem exists. It does not pinpoint where it is coming from. My goal is to make Your Opportunity River map a never-ending source of clarity to where the problems are happening, along with the strategies to resolve them and make sure they do not happen again.

With inventory, Frank's purchasing team did their best

to keep materials in stock well in advance of when the materials were needed. Yet somehow, a handful of necessary materials were either not available when production started or missing when it was time to ship the product. Additionally, schedulers for each product line provided due dates for orders, but because manufacturing information was maintained in spreadsheets, supervisors spent endless time walking the shop floor to find out the status of any given order. The same could be said about customer service. They were essentially flying blind, oblivious to where any production order was in the shop. Their method of helping customers was heading out to the shop floor and walking around to find out the status.

The organization was in perpetual firefighting mode. Shop floor supervisors were constantly putting out fires as their main daily function. Shop floor workers were moved from one priority to another, too often without finishing what they started. Customers were not getting their products and regularly showed their displeasure when calling into ABC Fab for status updates—further tying up staff in the office.

The most frustrating thing for Frank was that he could not understand how his internal processes were this complicated. He remembered times in the past when problems didn't exhaust the energy of his entire team. In the twenty-first century, it should be possible to indicate which parts of an order would ship first, and it should be easier to make adjustments when the customer updated an order. It should be possible to keep track of every item in inventory and to track progress across entire orders. But for ABC Fab—and for many manufacturers—that clarity was simply absent.

FLOW LEADS TO HIGHER PROFITS

These were not individual problems. Instead, they all related to one source: flow. Frank knew that *something* was slowing down the flow of his processes—he just didn't know what. Orders were pouring in faster than ever before, yet revenue was being blocked, slowing to what seemed to be a trickle, while profits were dwindling.

Flow is the speed and efficiency with which you deliver your products to your customers. Product orders flow through the back office—from sales, to engineering, inventory, and purchasing. They flow through planning and scheduling and out to the shop floor to production, shipping, and invoicing. The faster the flow, the more efficiently the organization runs, and the more profits reach the end of the river.

Despite all the complexity of his problems, it all came down to the fact that Frank's river wasn't flowing the way he expected. In fact, it had been stacking up for so long that when manufacturing needed steel, the material handlers could not find what they needed. So they just picked what was close and slightly larger to provide manufacturing. Unfortunately, that inventory was needed elsewhere and was now gone. That meant more replacement material had to be purchased, slowing down how quickly the next order could flow through production, while the needed material sat idle with no destination in sight.

Material handlers are robbing Peter to pay Paul. WIP inventory was building. There was no room for it, so the good parts that were waiting for other parts to be cut had to be sent back to the warehouse. Those parts were being picked for other stalled orders. By the time the backlogged parts had been cut, those sent to the warehouse were missing.

Each delay slowed the flow and tied up more cash. The invoices were also delayed, so there was less money to pay the bills. With less money to pay the bills, the only relief was the line of credit at the bank—but that, too, robbed ABC Fab of profits.

Instead of seeing this as chaos, once Frank could envision these issues as interrelated and connected to flow, he could see a path forward. If he wanted a mighty, efficient, and profitable Opportunity River, he had to expose the obstacles reducing flow across his operations.

To do that, he needed his Opportunity River map.

Right now, your map shows your river and all its tributaries. It gives you some clarity on revenue and production time. Now we can add new clarity about where obstructions creep into back office processes from the moment you take an order to the moment the product is shipped.

Before we do that, though, we need to understand the types of obstructions that are slowing down your internal operations and costing you money.

GETTING THE BENDS

Imagine you are traveling down a river on a kayak. You look ahead and see your river has a bend to the left. As you get to the bend, the scene opens up, and you see another river just on the other side of yours, running parallel to the one you're on. Between the rivers, you see a tree on a thin patch of land separating the rivers. The tree is immense and dwarfs everything else around it. It's a beautiful sight. What a great place! After the bend you paddle along with the lazy current for another half an hour. You take one bend after another and enjoy the view. Suddenly, just ahead you spy another giant tree dwarfing all the others—this time on your right.

Wait, that isn't a new tree. It's the same tree you saw just thirty minutes ago!

It turns out this river bends so much that it's brought you all the way back to where you started. While it would have taken fifteen seconds to pick up your kayak and walk across the narrow strip of land, you wasted thirty minutes rowing.

That's the danger of bends. In a river, they slow down flow and increase the time it takes to get where you're going.

In your business, they do the same thing—and they burn up time and cost you money. The scary part is that people are not trained to spot inefficiencies, so they see the extra steps as their job.

Rivers are often surprisingly easy to bend. The Red River, which is on the border between North Dakota and Minnesota, is full of bends. If you view it from the air, it seems as though you could travel forever and get nowhere.

The least bit of disruption and a little time is all it takes to create a bend in a river. Once a bend starts, the change in the river's current will continue to make the bend longer and longer. While it requires a significant amount of time, adding a bend to such a waterway can start as innocently as a river otter choosing to burrow a den on one bank instead of the other.

In the same way, seemingly minor individual decisions in a company's Opportunity River can lead to a massive restructuring of the whole river, without anyone noticing. They happen so slowly and continuously that most companies don't even notice the problem—until one day they look up and notice that one department or another cannot keep up.

Often bends develop through hiring. When ABC Fab was growing quickly, everyone felt the company was heading in the right direction. To handle the new workload, leadership hired people from XYZ Metals and LMN Structures. This seemed like a smart move. They were hiring energetic, competent people with experience. But left unattended, the new hires wore down processes at ABC. Bends created more bends—until the results of the process destruction became obvious.

None of these bends were purposeful or malevolent. New hires came in and made seemingly small changes that collectively caused major problems down the line. One shop floor manager used to work for XYZ. When he looked over the internal processes at ABC, he noticed that ABC happened to require management sign-off when changing the priority and order of projects on the floor. At XYZ, they'd allowed the team on the floor to make these calls for themselves. So, the new shop floor manager adjusted the process for his team at ABC.

To him, this just made more sense. It's how he'd been trained. It worked better for him. But his decision led to cascading changes that eventually created significant inefficiency across the business.

That's all it takes to create an obstruction—a small change without any desire to create a problem. This shop floor manager most likely thought they were being helpful. They likely assumed that their changes would speed up all projects. From their individual, biased perspective, these were better processes…but were they really better? And because ABC lacked clear boundaries to lock their process in, these changes were allowed to occur without any pushback—or even without any notice.

Whether caused by neglect or an effort to "shake things up," these bends force your river out of shape. And they can be located anywhere in the organization.

BENDS CREATE BIGGER PROBLEMS

When processes are otherwise running smoothly, a small bend isn't too much of a problem. Consider the bend the former XYZ manager created at ABC. If the vast majority of orders go unchanged and everyone follows ABC Fab's processes, it's a minor inconvenience. Certainly, it would be nice to remove it and speed things up slightly, but it's not worth too much attention.

This is often how bends are perceived. You might be aware that your order-taking process is a bit slow or there's a minor buildup of orders for certain parts. But the assumption is "that's business." You have bigger problems to worry about.

Unfortunately, bends have a way of growing and multiplying until they create massive issues for your company. In fact, when they aren't cleared up, they can create major obstructions that slow the process down to a crawl. When the process slows, orders in the department back up and that portion of the river holds more revenue than they can possibly handle. The result is lost time as that department reaches flood stage, while profits are draining away.

DAMS AND RESERVOIRS

While bends in the river slow down the flow of revenue in Your Opportunity River, another obstacle can stop the flow altogether and create backlogs. Dams can happen anywhere in your river. The most common dam is overworked individuals on your team. The workers who get dammed up are usually some of your best—those willing to take on anything and wear multiple hats. Because they're overworked, though, they can dam up your river, only allowing a trickle to get past them to flow down the river. If you have a small team of engineers and the engineer-to-order volume is high enough, the team can create a dam.

The result is a reservoir: the backlog of orders that pool up and stop flowing down the river.

For Frank, buyers were flooding the company with more inventory than could be effectively managed. Facing more work than they could handle, the material handlers became the dam. As a result, a reservoir of inventory became another obstruction in the flow of his Opportunity River.

Not every dam and reservoir is specific to the team. Every manufacturer has a bottlenecked machine on the shop floor that acts as a dam. It sets the pace of the operations downstream from the machine. Any work that gets ahead of the machine is an excellent example of a reservoir.

Another example is data analysis. There's nothing wrong with analysis—in fact, it's often central to best practices. However, with the wrong software, this process can often take so long that by the time the data is entered into spreadsheets, it's already obsolete. The time invested in compiling, entering, and analyzing information ends up slowing down the release of work to the shop without any additional benefit.

Dams and reservoirs can slow down and back up your river anywhere in your operations. And remember, these obstructions are not the result of individual mistakes; rather, they come from an inefficient process that limited the abilities of people to keep up. In fact, people are often the ones to suffer most. Being part of a dam is a major cause of stress for many of your best people, resulting in frustrations, excessive hours of work, a poor work/life balance, and the erosion of their health. It is imperative that companies find these obstructions, because left unattended, employees will burn out quickly.

WHIRLPOOLS

While the obstacles addressed earlier will definitely impact the flow of Your Opportunity River, the obstacles that are often the hardest to see can be the most dangerous to your bottom line. These are whirlpools. As you know, a whirlpool swirls and sucks in anything that comes into its vortex. Fill a sink and pull the plug. You will see a whirlpool that sucks water down the drain. When a whirlpool develops in your river, it is not sucking the water. It is sucking the revenue that should flow down to the main river as profits for your company.

Here is an example of whirlpools cleverly hidden every-where in an organization. In 2022, *Harvard Business Review* did a study called "How Much Time and Energy Do We Waste Toggling Between Applications" that reviewed whirl-pools, or what they called "operational taxes" companies unknowingly pay. The authors noted, "Toggling is often dismissed as simply 'how we work now,' even though it's also taxing for people and a waste of time, effort, and focus."

The authors referred to the problem as a "toggling tax." In their analysis, they monitored 137 individuals across many departments in three different companies for a period of five weeks. They found that the average user toggled between different apps and websites nearly 1,200 times each day, losing just under four hours a week reorienting them-selves after toggling between apps. That amounted to a loss of five working weeks per person over the course of a year.

Whirlpools often develop around other obstructions. Frank's reservoir of inventory created a whirlpool that con-sumed excess cash that could have been put to better use elsewhere in the organization. It sucked up a considerable amount of material and consumed the time of material handlers, while also taking space in the warehouse—all of which drained profits from the organization. Turning to the business's line of credit to finance the inventory threw more money into the whirlpool. When it comes time to count the inventory, that extra effort also falls into the whirlpool.

Whirlpools don't stop there. One of the largest whirlpools

in most manufacturing organizations is paper. Everywhere paper exists—whether reports, production paperwork, accounting information, etc.—it is sucking up resources. It takes time to print, time to distribute, time to wade through, time to find when it is misplaced, all when, in many cases, the information printed on the paper is quickly obsolete. In the end, you throw it all away.

Consider production paperwork. Packets of paper are printed by your staff. Drawings are printed, along with routers, bills-of-material, quality information, work instructions, pick lists, and so on. All that paper is sorted, packed into clear plastic envelopes, and sent out to the shop floor by the hundreds and thousands. Those on the shop floor must wade through the volume of packets to determine what to work on next and wade through the stack of paper in a packet to find just enough information for them to do their job. When the customer or your engineering department makes a change, some or all of the packets must be reprinted. In that case, the old packets need to be found somewhere floating around in the shop, trashed, and replaced with the new ones. Too often, the changes get to the shop floor too late to save parts. That creates scrap or rework. All these functions are waste and happen every single day in manufacturing.

Whirlpools don't stop on their own, and they will suck in everything if you aren't careful. They will consume your time, your attention, your patience, your materials, your flow, and as much revenue as ever gets close enough to snatch.

If left unaddressed, whirlpools and other obstructions can cost you more than profit margins. They can cost your whole business.

REMOVING YOUR OBSTACLES

Obstacles increase the risk of flooding and leave your profits pouring over the banks of Your Opportunity River in good times, while they increase the risk droughts will dry up all your resources and put your business under additional pressure in the tough times.

The ultimate challenge for manufacturers is how to increase the height of your riverbanks, allowing your company to run more efficiently and more profitably at higher revenue levels without flooding. At the same time, you want to lower your overhead, reducing the risk of severe drought, without investing another dime in people, inventory, machinery, or facilities. To do that, you have to find a way to grow revenue and make more profits, without increasing overhead. Doing so would also lower your breakeven point to better weather droughts.

But how? How do you turn floods into an opportunity and droughts into a manageable inconvenience?

Flow, of course. You improve flow to increase the speed of operations and raise your capacity. And improving flow is as simple as finding and removing those obstacles that are currently in your way.

Scan now for a quick video summary of this chapter!

Dive into key insights in seconds.

https://qrco.de/yor31nz7

SCAN HERE

SEEKING OUT OBSTRUCTIONS

OBSTRUCTIONS ARE TOO OFTEN AMAZINGLY WELL hidden, resulting from years and years of doing the same procedures in the same way. Years ago, ABC Fab required accounting to create job cards to capture all the time and materials needed to manufacture a product. Back then, the company just cut steel to make piece parts and fabricated weldments to customer requirements. The shop floor workers would manually fill out their time and the materials used on the job cards as the job manually worked its way through the shop. The accounting staff put the job card process in place to capture the detailed labor, material, and outsourced services cost, then totaled the numbers together and factored in some overhead to determine the total cost for the product. That would give the company an idea of how much profit was made.

Back in those days, the company was relatively small, and their outdated process worked well for accounting. At the same time, the accounting process did little to benefit manufacturing. There was no scheduling, capacity planning, utilization, or efficiency information to support manufacturing operations. Those in manufacturing determined how to get work through the shop by having daily meetings. There was no such thing as spreadsheets in those days, so meetings and magnetic scheduling boards were the main method of prioritizing the work. After some growth in the company, meetings were taking too much time away from production as the fabricators on the shop floor sat in on those meetings.

As the years went by, the volume of orders grew substantially, along with the complexity of products, and the meetings became overwhelming. How did this happen? Actually, it happens way too often in companies where accounting makes decisions based on the simplest way to gather costs for the benefit of accounting and the creation of financial statements. Such a practice is what I call "accounting-driven."

In an accounting-driven practice, by prioritizing accounting and not manufacturing needs, there can be no scheduling of jobs through various work centers, which leads to more shop floor meetings, while losing visibility for managers to see problems in manufacturing. The magnetic scheduling boards showed where the work was at, yet everyone downstream was oblivious to what jobs they should work on until told by managers.

Think of this process like putting an empty bucket in the tributary and as it flows downstream, workers put their time and materials information into it. But the bucket is floating downstream at the whim of the current in the river and not according to the manufacturing requirements of the individual parts being made. Nobody can account for the bucket until it finishes flowing through manufacturing and is collected by the accounting team. In the meantime, manufacturing isn't operating to a cohesive plan, but rather to the squeaky wheel principle, giving priority to the customer who yells the loudest.

Let's compare that practice to a "manufacturing-driven organization" where every part is routed and scheduled to the required locations in the shop to make the part. All parts were cut, then some were bent, others rolled, some drilled, and even some with combinations of these operations, in addition to welding, prep, and painting. At each step of the manufacturing process, workers charge their time and required materials into the ERP system. Jobs are scheduled through the shop based on the available capacities of each work center. Every work center knows what jobs are coming their way and which have priority over the others. It is easy to collect time and material information at every step and managers have full visibility to where jobs are at, without the need for any shop floor meetings.

In the accounting-driven organization, managers never know the status of the job until it is complete, unless someone walks around and locates the job card(s) associated with the job. Jobs cannot be scheduled, only prioritized. The meeting process to sort out and prioritize jobs becomes a dam that holds back production until the next meeting, while the job cards represent the reservoir of work that is waiting to be performed. The meetings with managers and workers are whirlpools of idle people and machinery that are slowing the flow of work through the shop and eating profits from the organization.

Frank knew such an accounting-driven organization could not sustain itself as the company continued to grow. The old practice was what kept the company small. The lost utilization of people and machinery due to constant meetings kept the banks of the river low, resulting in flood stage occurring way too easily and too often.

THE END OF BUSINESS AS USUAL

Accounting-driven companies and even accounting-driven ERP systems are, to this day, still too often the norm in manufacturing companies. Think about it. Accounting-driven systems may add up all the costs and provide good financial statements, but none of them will be able to promise an accurate customer delivery date for their order, much less optimize inventory and the shop floor to deliver the product on time.

This is another one of those obstructions we covered in the last chapter that, if you are not looking for them, are invisible. They hide under the surface, as part of your "business as usual" assumptions.

To go any further, you'll need to abandon that expression. "Business as usual" hides all the bends that increase the length of your tributaries and slow the flow of the river. It increases the amount of cash needed to fund the process. Those bends can flow into massive reservoirs, held back by dams that stop the flow and create backlogs in orders, inventory, manufacturing, and more, while in each of these obstacles, whirlpools are lurking that consume lazy and inefficient use of time, resources, and cash. If you don't remove them now, they will cost you.

Only after every activity of your internal processes is open to investigation and review can you begin to see where "business as usual" is actually "business as inefficiency."

START AT THE BEGINNING

To find your obstructions, you have to start by recognizing that this is a process. You will not find every bend on first inspection. The aim is to run through this process now and to repeat it forever. You and your team will get better at catching obstacles as you go.

That said, your aim on this first review is to catch the biggest obstacles, the low-hanging fruit. Look for the most significant and widespread obstacles that are dramatically reducing the flow of Your Opportunity River. You want to find those obstacles and straighten them to get the river flowing faster.

Again, this does not need to be an exhaustive assessment of your operations. They should be fairly obvious. Here, we're looking for those issues that you and others in the past have noted. These are the things that have concerned or frustrated you—the sort of problems dismissed as "business as usual."

REVIEWING A WHOLE TRIBUTARY

As you review your internal operations, I suggest you start at the taking of a sales order and go through to shipping the product to the customer of your largest tributary. As you will notice, the estimating process is not included in our focus on laying out tributaries. The reason is simple. While estimating is a key component of a manufacturing business, creating an estimate for a prospective or current customer does not always result in a sales order.

Flood stage happens as a result of taking sales orders, most of which requires an estimate, yet far too many estimates do not result in a sales order. In fact, most manufacturers win, on average, from 8 percent to 20 percent of their estimates. That means 80 to 92 percent of estimates do not contribute to the revenue flowing down Your Opportunity River.

Being more efficient in the estimating process is a hot topic and a discussion all its own, but with our focus on incoming orders revenue, it is not one we will cover in this book.

We are concentrating on the operational impact of the 8 to 20 percent that become sales orders and create revenue flowing down the entire tributary. At this point, you should focus on the entire tributary to determine back office and shop floor operational obstructions happening along the entire fulfillment process: from sales order entry to engineering (if applicable), creating your manufacturing routings and bills-of-materials, planning and scheduling, inventory control, purchasing, creating paperwork, releasing jobs to the shop floor, production, quality, shipping, and accounting/invoicing.

Label each area clearly along your tributary. If it helps, you can draw lines through the tributary to segment it more effectively. I suggest you make tick marks along your river, as shown in the illustration, to indicate the various departments. I would suggest breaking the tributary down into equal segments, one for each area or department in the overall fulfillment process.

FOCUS ON THE BACK OFFICE

You might notice that most of the functions listed are not in the area of production but rather back office operations. There's a good reason for this. If you ask most COOs, they'll say their shop floor has more capacity than the back office can effectively support. In other words, the office can be like the governor on a golf cart, limiting the speed, throughput, and capacity of production. There are a lot of reasons for this, like changing priorities, lack of necessary production information, flooding the shop with job packets, etc. That's one of the key insights of mapping Your Opportunity River obstructions: often, the biggest obstacle to manufacturing is the back office itself!

After fifty years in manufacturing and witnessing the operations of hundreds and hundreds of manufacturers, I can tell you that the ability of the shop to produce is dependent on the ability of the back office to support the shop. Yet, the shop gets huge investments in new machinery and equipment, leaving the back office with accounting software and way too many spreadsheets. Streamline the back office, and both the back office and the shop will reap considerable gains.

That's not to say obstructions don't happen on the shop floor. They do! However, the back office usually plays a much bigger part in limiting the flow through manufacturing, and that needs to be your initial focus. And sometimes, you fix the back office operations, and mysteriously, the obstructions on the shop floor go away all by themselves.

FIND THE WASTE AND TRACE IT BACK

As you review the process along each tributary, it's time to do a gut check. If you feel like the flow of the river through any particular department is slower than you think it should be, then put a squiggly line in the tributary to show suspected bends. Next to the indicator, label what function and department you feel is causing the problem. This will make each obstacle easier to understand as your drawing gets busier. If you feel like any department, function, or even a person has more work than they can handle—and if they have a backlog of work waiting behind them—draw a rectangle across the tributary to indicate a dam. Since a dam always creates a reservoir, draw an oval or circle immediately upstream from the dam to indicate a reservoir. You may want to consider putting a potential dollar amount or range of dollars for each obstacle, meaning how much revenue the obstacle is holding back. Another option is to put a restaurant menu price indicator of a single dollar sign for a small impact, all the way to four dollar signs for a significant obstacle.

Understand that there is no blame when labeling an obstruction. Our aim is simply to recognize where work must be done to improve flow. We have to remain unbiased about the causes at this point. Many times, dams will result not from an individual holding back the flow but from functions upstream that overload the individual's work. You would never find the initial source of the obstruction—or be able to remove it—if you immediately blamed those at the dam site for the creation of a dam.

For instance, you might find a huge dam around what work should get priority in production. The immediate team under suspicion would be your team of floor supervisors, who too often are making these calls. But if you look further up the tributary, you might find that engineers might be completing their work based on the priority to do the engineering and not on how the product will be built. If job packets are routinely created when engineering finishes their work, the result will be launching many low-priority job packets into the shop—creating a reservoir of information and an increase in WIP. This forces supervisors and machine operators to sift through hundreds of packets and determine which should be started in production.

MAKING YOUR WHIRLPOOLS

Now it is time to look for whirlpools. There are a number of culprits to watch for. As you survey your tributary, look for signs of whirlpools particularly around your other obstructions. These might include holding costs due to excess inventory, the inherent inefficiencies of paperwork, manipulating data for the use with offline spreadsheets, endless searching for documents and the lack of information, and bends due to slower or complex processes and the resulting time delays of the longer river.

You can also look out on the shop floor, watching for idle machines waiting for inventory; spikes in poor quality caused by the lack of information; machine maintenance increases due to skipping routine maintenance to catch up on production; and so on. When companies have a lot of revenue running down their Opportunity River, the overload causes confusion, resulting in way too many meetings to sort out what needs to be done. Remember, if a thirty-minute meeting has six people in it, it results in three hours of lost time. If sixteen people are in the meeting, it burns up eight hours of time, never to be available again.

Label your tributaries with a spiral over the area of the tributary where you see any potential whirlpool exists, and put a name on the whirlpool. In any company, there are more whirlpools than can possibly be imagined. They represent the hidden costs of inefficiency that are devouring cash in more ways than possibly expected.

And remember, whirlpools are often invisible upon first look, so keep your eyes open for any signs one is consuming your resources near any obstacle.

WATCH FOR FLOODING

With your obstacles roughly charted, review the same tributary in periods of flooding. As you'll recall, you reach flood stage when high revenues overwhelm areas of your company with work and your profits spill over the banks of Your Opportunity River. Ideally, this revenue would flow rapidly down your tributaries without spilling over the banks to be collected as profits at the end of your river.

Flooding can be found anywhere and everywhere in the organization, but it will almost certainly occur at the location of obstructions. At flood stage, a bend can go from a minor slowdown to an internal crisis. A whirlpool will suck down more materials, time, mind share, and revenue as you try to catch up, fix defective products, rush order missing parts, etc.

But flooding can equally cause new bends, dams, reservoirs, and whirlpools. Orders coming in unbelievably fast (when it rains, it pours) makes it impossible to handle the load. Mistakes happen anywhere and everywhere. It takes constant firefighting to get anything through the back office and shop. Your team is highly stressed and working overtime, delivery dates are missed, customers are angry, and priorities are constantly changing.

Where you find an area of consistent flooding, draw a wavy line on both sides of the tributary in the respective departments. If the entire tributary is flooded, draw the wavy lines along the entire tributary.

EXPAND TO EVERY TRIBUTARY

At this point, the map of your main tributary with all the obstacles you detect is done. It is time to expand to the next tributary. Run through your second-largest product line and seek out the obstacles.

This should be much easier since most manufacturers have consistent practices, so many obstacles will repeat in other tributaries. For example, if there's a problem with all the paper running through your largest tributary, it is good to assume the same problem will exist in the next one.

Still, keep an eye out for unique bends, dams, reservoirs, and whirlpools that might develop in each product line. Is there a sourcing issue for one particular set of products? Do the customers for one product line make more change orders than other product lines? Do some product lines have better internal procedures than others? With some looking around, you might find procedures used in other parts of the organization that are more effective in resolving issues in other tributaries.

It's also important to look for the unexpected: a truly successful tributary. Many times, there are product lines that have what I like to refer to as "The Perfect Order," referring to a customer order that flows quickly and smoothly through your internal operations and through the shop with no delays and no interruptions, in minimal time. The strategy here is to make as many product orders as possible "The Perfect Order."

KEEP UPDATING YOUR TRIBUTARIES

As I mentioned at the beginning of the chapter, you won't catch every obstacle on the first review. This process should become a habit—and I will explain why later. You should review this process monthly to check in on how the flow of each of the tributaries is improving, as well as noting any new obstacles that show up. By doing this monthly, you will be tracking the process in line with your accounting periods and will see how all your processes react or respond to varying levels of revenue. You will also observe optimum levels of performance, as well as when the process is particularly strained.

As you do this, be sure to also put numbers behind your changes. In Chapter 2, we discussed indicating your revenue and, if known, your profit and profit percentage at the end of each tributary. Monitor these using a monthly financial statement supporting schedule from your ERP system. Also record monthly net income from your income statement. These measures will provide you with feedback that you are managing obstacles and making improvements in profitability. These improvements are raising the banks of your river beyond the revenue levels where, in the past, they were eroding. Going through this monthly is fast and keeps you on top of issues before they create havoc in the organization.

Over time, you will be able to predict when you will go into flood stage and drought by watching your bookings (dollar value of orders taken). The hidden secret is to measure the difference in revenue between flood stage and drought. Our intent is to widen that range of optimum profitability as widely as possible.

This method of widening the range of optimum profitability leverages improved efficiency as compared to adding more people, inventory, machinery, and facilities. When adding resources, you increase overhead in the organization, requiring more revenue to cover these higher costs. The higher costs increase the drought stage breakeven revenue, making it harder to earn a profit when business is not so good. On the other hand, when you optimize your existing resources by removing profit-eating obstacles, you are making your internal operations run more efficiently, which lowers your breakeven point. The goal is to raise the banks of the tributary to take on more revenue, while lowering the bottom of the tributary to run the company profitably at lower revenue levels.

Obviously, you want to know as far in advance as possible when flood stage will happen so you can develop strategies to limit any potential profit loss and chaos. At the same time, tracking these numbers will allow you to generate metrics to prove the solutions in this book will be raising the riverbanks to prevent flooding and widen the profitable revenue range to reduce the risk of droughts.

If you don't do this, the complexity of the obstacles will eventually overrun your organization's ability to handle them without immense amounts of time and attention. For Frank, over time, as profits eroded, the obstacles became "business as usual." He was praised by management for $100,000 additional profit, which he knew was only 1.1 percent of the additional $9 million in revenue. If ABC Fab's normal profit margin was 8 percent, the profit should have been $720,000, a loss of $620,000. If their normal margin was 12 percent, the profit should have been $1,080,000. In other words, ABC's obstructions resulted not in a small gain but a loss of $980,000 in profit. Such profit margins are possible in manufacturing—if you remove the obstacles from your processes.

Now that you know where your obstacles are, you can regain that profitability. But first, you will have to remove each of the obstacles in your way.

Scan now for a quick video summary of this chapter!

Dive into key insights in seconds.

https://qrco.de/yor4c5ne

CHAPTER 5

STRAIGHTEN YOUR OPPORTUNITY RIVER

WITH THE GOAL OF MAKING YOUR BUSINESS AS profitable as possible, the first step to accomplishing that is to remove the obstructions. You want to:

- Straighten the bends
- Remove the dams
- Empty the reservoirs
- Maximize the flow to eliminate whirlpools
- Increase the height of the banks to reduce/eliminate flooding
- Dredge the river bottom to reduce the impact of droughts

Each of these objectives leads to a river that is straighter and flows at a faster rate. When bends are straightened, internal operations are more efficient, and orders flow faster. When dams are removed strategically (as opposed to blown up, which would lead to flooding downriver), the reservoirs empty in a controlled manner—creating increased profitability at a rate you can handle. By straightening the bends, removing the dams, and emptying the reservoirs, you will also eliminate the associated whirlpools.

When these obstacles are removed, you will find that flooding happens less often, and you are more resistant to droughts—because your internal operations are more efficient. At this point, your operations truly become *Your* Opportunity River. As in nature, you remove the obstacles in a river, and it instantly flows faster.

With the clarity of Your Opportunity River map, this can be so much simpler than it seemed before. As a kid, did you ever see standing water that was blocked from flowing? Perhaps some mud had accumulated in the path of a little stream, or some ice was blocking the way. Yet, because you could see the obstacle, all you had to do was clear away the mud or break up that ice for the water to flow smoothly again.

Removing the obstacles in Your Opportunity River has the same result. When obstacles are removed, nothing holds the profits and production back. They flow smoothly and quickly. In fact, all the new machinery you have purchased will now be better utilized, which reduces the lead time in your shop. As a result, Your Opportunity River can now handle greater revenue without hitting flood stage or suffering droughts—and that means stability, efficiency, profit, and a massive amount of potential you can unlock for the future.

What if Your Opportunity River has a reservoir filled with rising inventory levels? We all know that more inventory carries more costs—requiring more space, more material handling, more cycle counts, longer physical inventories, and tying up more cash (or a line of credit). You can now trace the source of such issues and remove the obstacles that are slowing it down.

And once you get started on this process, it gets easier every time you do it. Fixing one obstacle will often expose others that have gone unnoticed.

FRANK FINDS HIS OBSTACLES

Frank knew that ABC Fab had a flow issue. After mapping his obstacles, he knew he had to concentrate on one obstacle at a time. He determined which obstacle appeared to be creating the greatest havoc for the company and set priorities to remove it from his main tributary. Before he began, he made a point of labeling the priorities for each obstacle. The highest-priority obstacle on the tributary was number one, then the next severe obstacle became number two, and so on.

Frank's biggest obstacle was in purchasing and storing

materials. Material-related issues created bends, dams, whirlpools, and flooding along the entire river.

But how was Frank going to remove those obstacles? Daily meetings were held to determine what could be done and come up with new priorities. But where to start?

In order to solve his problem, Frank had to start by asking the question "Why?" with the main obstacle in mind. When seeking the source of an obstacle, it is always best to start upstream as far as possible, because issues like those at ABC Fab tend to flow downstream. Frank started with the purchasing team and asked, "Why do we have so much inventory?" The answer was immediate: "That's how we've always done it." Frank already knew that wasn't a good enough reason, so he asked, "Why have we always done it that way?" This time, he was met with silence. Eventually, someone suggested he speak to Susan, who the team thought had started the practice fifteen years ago and was now retired.

Generally, if you ask five whys, you will get to the root of most problems. So, Frank dutifully pushed forward. He asked, "Why would Susan have loaded the warehouse with materials?" Now, there was a bit more thinking. One person on the purchasing team suggested, "Over the years, we have been taught that if we want to keep our jobs, never run out of inventory." After some serious thought, Frank asked, "But why are the materials here so far in advance of when they are needed?" There was some discussion among the team. The answer made perfect sense: "We are told by our scheduler when we need the material, and we arrange to get it here by those dates."

Frank had exhausted his whys, so he changed the approach to dig deeper: "How good is our scheduler at providing manufacturing dates that we can hit?" Frank cut right to the bone with that question. Everyone on the purchasing team looked at one another, and one responded, "When we aren't very busy, the scheduler is pretty good. But when we get really busy, he can't possibly keep up with the load, much less the changing demand. He's put us in a situation in which we don't know if we are producing faster than his dates or slower. As a result, we get the materials here as soon as possible, just in case."

Frank went right to the scheduler and asked how he was coming up with dates. "Honestly," the scheduler told him, "not well. For the last eight to twelve months, our customers have been buying on scarcity knowing we have long lead times and wanting to get a spot in the schedule before the lead times get even longer. When they place an order, I give them a due date. Then, a few days later, they come back and increase the quantity—but they still want the same delivery date! It is so overwhelming. I can't keep up. So, I've gone from promising delivery in four weeks, to five weeks, and now we're at four months. But I really don't know how long it will take."

With a little more probing, it all clicked. Frank realized the problem did not come down to incompetence from his scheduler—it was something far simpler. The reason for the advanced purchases was because the scheduler set due dates for sales using a spreadsheet. Creating a reasonably accurate schedule could not be done fast enough with the volume of incoming orders by using a spreadsheet. As a result, the scheduler was just guesstimating due dates by guesstimating the backlog. The delivery date promises made to customers were impossible to meet, yet purchasing used the promises that flooded the warehouse with materials.

Frank asked why the scheduler had to rely so heavily on a basic spreadsheet. They paid a lot of money for their ERP system. Why weren't they using it for scheduling? The answer was not what Frank wanted to hear. The scheduler said he was very proficient with spreadsheets. He was uncomfortable with the ERP software, so he stuck with what he knew. Unfortunately for the scheduler, sales could not get data downloaded fast enough into spreadsheets, much less update them with what production completed. The spreadsheets became an obstacle blocking progress down the river. Put under the stress of a flood of orders, the scheduler had created an unintended dam in the organization that generated inventory and slowed down everything downstream.

Finally, Frank was at the source of his problems. The scheduler and others in the organization were creating all sorts of workarounds, resulting in the creation of more bends, dams, and reservoirs that caused flooding in much of the organization, and at times, droughts in manufacturing. No wonder Frank was earning a paltry 1.1 percent profit from $9 million in new revenue!

THE ROOT CAUSE OF EVERY OBSTACLE

Frank's obstacles were not uncommon in manufacturing. Many obstacles relate to planning and scheduling. Since those two functions directly impact other departments in the organization, an obstacle there has a ripple effect, like throwing a rock into a calm pond. In Frank's situation, the ripples fanned through the entire organization. Once Frank was at the source of the obstacle, he could trace ripples as far as sales and customer service, where his teams were impacted by customers constantly calling to get updates on their orders and pushing to become a higher priority. Since only so much can be done in a day, the time spent on these calls limited the sales team's ability to enter new orders. That created bends in the river, slowing down the process. The fact is, the time spent on customer satisfaction issues had sales and customer service asking for two additional full-time workers. Such an investment could have burned up most of the $100,000 extra profit in under a year.

Such ripples can be far reaching, further complicating the search for the initial source of the obstacle. How can you find that source and eliminate it?

To help in this goal, we can simplify what you should be searching for. While obstacles can be bends, dams, reservoirs, etc., when you look into the details behind the obstacles, they all have common root causes. In fact, with very few exceptions, they are caused by just three sources. Those are:

- Resources (people, inventory, machinery, facilities)
- Processes
- Technology

Sometimes the obstacles are the result of one of the sources, other times two, or even all three. Yet, they all come down to these or a combination of these.

Take Frank's scheduler. He was using spreadsheets that he had no ability to keep updated with new orders or the results of production. Trying to keep those updated meant manually running programs to download information from the ERP system and upload it into spreadsheets, or worse yet, manually entering it.

Here, we can see all three forces at work. There was a technology element in the use of spreadsheets over the ERP. There was a process problem in the manual inputting of data that couldn't keep up with production. But ultimately, the source of the obstacle was a resource. The scheduler was uncomfortable with the ERP system and made the choice to rely on spreadsheets. Does that mean the scheduler was a bad employee? Not at all. But he had made a poor decision about the tools he would use for the job. And that made him the root cause of Frank's problem.

To fix this issue, all Frank had to do was push that mound of mud out of the way to let his river flow straight again. He talked to his scheduler, signed him up for training on the ERP system, and locked that process in place for the company.

Suddenly, results improved. Scheduling was more up-to-date, orders ran more smoothly, and profits increased. Frank addressed the root cause, and the entire river benefited.

Scan now for a quick video summary of this chapter!

Dive into key insights in seconds.

https://qrco.de/yor5uVCy

CHAPTER 6

OPEN THE FLOOD GATES

THE SOURCE OF YOUR OBSTACLES IS ALMOST ALWAYS in your resources, the internal processes, and/or the level of technology in your organization. You may never have seen it put that way, but instinctively, you know this is true. If I asked you what your most important asset was, most of you would tell me it was your resources. Without them, you wouldn't have a business. And when orders come in faster than they can be handled, what is the first response? To increase your people resources. This can happen by working more hours, adding more shifts, etc.

Other options to handle flooding include increasing inventory, adding facilities, or buying more machines. All of these are efforts to deal with increasing levels of internal complexity.

What if there was another option available?

Consider those new machines. Most owners and COOs in manufacturing have an extensive knowledge of what happens on the shop floor. Many will also admit their ignorance of the details associated with what happens in the back office. So when they're looking for a way to reduce flooding, it makes sense that the solution they reach for is a new, state-of-the-art machine.

Executives and managers can easily see how new machines can operate much faster and more accurately than older machinery. Often, a single new machine can do the work of multiple older machines. That machine, in theory, should improve the process by creating better parts faster—all while requiring fewer operators. Every manufacturing CEO can tell you how much better their new machine is for the shop because they can see it instantly with their own two eyes. Adding new machines will move products through the shop faster, but does that reduce the flooding? Not when machines aren't the problem.

Another alternative for improvements on the shop floor is moving machines around to work in cells. Why do this? Because they improve the process, reduce material handling, and improve quality, which are shop floor problems. But once again, while this normally nets some additional shop floor efficiency, it will not resolve deeper issues that are caused by obstacles originating in the back office.

The truth is back office challenges are often causing all the obstacles and leading to so much flooding. And to remove those obstacles, you can't rely on the old solutions.

The real solution must be found looking beyond the shop floor, in the area you likely spend the least amount of your time thinking about: the back office.

What if all along in your back office you had the same three gigantic pumps—resources, process, and technology (referred to as RPT going forward)—that you had never really optimized in the back office? What if those pumps could propel more revenue down all the tributaries of Your Opportunity River faster than ever before, removing every obstacle in their wake? And what if those pumps could also exponentially scale your company's sales and profits?

THE LAST PLACE YOU LOOK

To use these pumps, you have to first recognize the true impact your office has on production. While you see obstacles on the shop floor, as said too many times already, the source of the chaos is likely in the office. Your lower profits and limited growth are the result of working over, around, and through that chaos—which is just another term for the dams, reservoirs, bends, and whirlpools we've already discussed.

To optimize your organization, you need to optimize the mix of RPT in every department in your organization. This starts with your most important asset: your people. Just like the people on the shop floor, the people in your back office are your best resource. But when you hamper them with inefficient processes, they spend their time doing busy-work. When you limit the technology available to them, they spend all their time entering, reentering, and moving data from one place to another—from one spreadsheet to another or one database to another.

The most important thing you can do in your organization, then, is *optimize your back office personnel*. To do that, you have to move beyond the obvious solution. Instead of replacing them or adding new people to the office, first, streamline the processes by removing the obstacles, then simplify the processes people perform by automating them. That way, you can eliminate all the mindless busywork they do in the course of a day.

At this point, improving processes is really your only option—because bringing new people in is increasingly off the table. This book was written from 2022 to 2023, and for at least the last ten years, manufacturing—along with every other industry—was facing the same challenge: not enough qualified people. Every business competes on wages, benefits, and signing bonuses. Every business is on job boards and at job fairs—all in the effort to find people. Many of the people they hire never show up or leave within weeks of their first day. Others have limited skills, requiring expensive training.

Don't get me wrong, there are very good people out there, but there are also a lot of manufacturers out there. If you want to remove obstacles and open the flood gates to growth and profitability, you're going to have to use the process and technology pumps to harness the power of those people who are already in your company.

CREATING DAM BUSTERS

What if you could make your back office team into super-powered dam busters—people who could do so much more than they ever did before that they blow through the obstacles in their path? Just think about the potential. If they could do more than they ever did before, it would free up considerable amounts of time, resources, and money.

The key is automation, but not the sort you probably use right now. At the moment, you're probably like most manufacturers whose automation is to create a bunch of spreadsheets by manually entering information from a bunch of databases. Back office automation can do so much more.

Automation can transform the back office the same way all the newer machines you've bought have transformed the shop floor. Those machines turned your people on the floor into dam busters who could do more work with fewer people and fewer machines. Now, it's time to do the same thing with the back office that's still hitting flood stage.

When revenue is running over the banks of your river, your profits are spilling everywhere, all because the obstacles have clogged that section of your river. Time to blast it wide open.

The answer here is highly integrated ERP software that can eliminate much of the busywork that is holding your team back. For example, Advanced Planning and Scheduling (APS) can determine accurate delivery dates in seconds, while analyzing complex routings and bills-of-materials, current shop floor load and capacity, available materials, scheduled purchase order receipts, and vendor lead times down to each individual part, even across multiple facilities that source parts from one another. They can schedule work to optimize setups and run parts that need the same raw material together. Imagine how much easier it would be for your customer service team to enter orders and promise highly reliable delivery dates in seconds. Figuring that out on spreadsheets in real time is impossible, but APS can do it at the push of a button.

WELCOME TO WHITESPACE

By implementing automated technology to bust through your obstacles, you actually accomplish two important things. First, you flatline your people costs. No need to hire more people and no additional labor costs. Second, by automating much of their busywork, you create what I refer to as "organizational whitespace." This is a concept I've been developing since 1983.

At the time, I was analyzing the engineering department of a two-thousand-employee shipbuilding company. All of their drawings were done by hand with pencil, paper, and a drawing board. I did my due diligence and was ready to present the findings on a series of 3-D solid-model CAD workstations to the company's president and engineering manager, both of whom had far more experience in business than a twenty-something-year-old. When I mentioned the savings in time to the executives, the engineering manager's response was: "Tell us how you are saving this company money. We are going to spend over a million dollars on equipment to save time, but we are still going to pay those engineers and designers the same amount of money."

He had me on that one. I had no answer, and the company did nothing.

It took me a long time and a lot of thought to figure it out. The problem haunted me. But in the last ten or so years, I've worked it out—and the solution just so happens to address the number one issue manufacturers are struggling with.

Think about it this way. If you create organizational whitespace, you create people capacity. Each person can do more because they have fewer repetitive responsibilities. This can be such a powerful tool to drive your company to record revenues while increasing process efficiency—to such an extent you raise the banks of Your Opportunity River, protecting your company from flood stage throughout the organization.

When you find the best quality software in this area, it can be so powerful that—to paraphrase the entrepreneur and investor Daymond John—you can harvest significant value from all your internal resources (people, inventory, machinery, and facilities) without investing an additional dime in any one of them.

And that's the single biggest key to maximizing the flow of Your Opportunity River: to maximize whitespace through all your internal resources. At the same time, by flatlining people costs, you also flatline operational expenses, which means when a drought in the marketplace hits, your company will be in an optimal financial position.

Compare that position to those who hired more people, added more machinery, increased inventory, or added more facilities. Those result in the added expenses that push Your Opportunity River bottom higher. When overhead is high, it takes more revenue to keep the company afloat.

By maximizing flow while holding costs at bay, your company can still make money when the markets go flat. By increasing efficiency, you can lower inventory costs. Adding that onto the benefits of process, technology, and whitespace actually dredges the riverbed of Your Opportunity River by lowering your overhead, allowing you to thrive in drought situations, while competitors crumble and disappear.

But that's not to say that every ERP can provide these benefits. In fact, as you will see in Chapter 8, you need more than just an ERP system for your organization. Before we get there, though, let's cast our eyes forward to just where these ideas can take your company—if you can protect your river from invasive ecosystems.

SCAN HERE

Scan now for a quick video summary of this chapter!

Dive into key insights in seconds.

https://qrco.de/yor6uVCz

CHAPTER 7

MAKE YOUR OPPORTUNITY RIVER FOREVER GREEN

FOR THE FIRST TIME IN HIS LONG CAREER, FRANK could visualize all the pieces coming together across his organization and could grasp the overall strategy to further improvement. He and his team had mapped out their river system to show how the streams of revenue flowed together.

The team had also taken their river map and noted the obstacles on every tributary that were slowing the company down. Time and effort to resolve the obstacles were key, so the team focused on the low-hanging fruit first. They did the work to determine the root cause and the impact that rippled through other departments in the company. There were bends, dams, reservoirs, and profit-sucking whirlpools everywhere they looked—once they knew what they were looking for. Frank's team got to the bottom of the existing obstacles and found the unique mix of RPT in each area of their back office, correcting the internal issues to maximize the flow of revenue through the tributaries.

One of the miracles they found was most of the obstacles showed up across all of their product lines. Obstacles that impacted one product line, more often than not, seemed to flow through to others as well.

For ABC, all these developments meant the team finally had a greater appreciation for, and clarity on, their revenue streams, as well as the damaging impact obstacles had on their product line throughput and profits. Obstacles could appear anywhere, but the team was always looking out for them.

Ever since mapping out ABC's Opportunity River, Frank had the accounting group gathering monthly revenues, profits, and profit percentages of each tributary, along with net income of the company. By maintaining that information on a month-by-month basis, Frank could see the flow of revenue and profit levels by tributary (in ABC's situation, by product line). He now had crystal clarity on which product lines had strong profit margins and which lines saw their margins eroding from obstacles. More importantly, by watching those revenue and profit numbers fluctuate over time, Frank had the benchmarks he needed to monitor the return on investment for their improvements, and to be quickly aware of impending flood stage and drought for every tributary. If a problem surfaced, he engaged his team in locating the obstructions and proactively eliminating them. Frank's accounting team created financial analysis in their ERP system to make him aware of changing financial numbers. They also used their incoming order volumes to predict potential flood stage and drought conditions, giving them advanced visibility and time to respond.

ABC Fab had done a lot to optimize their internal operations, which set the stage to have forever green business improvements.

Yet new obstacles were becoming exposed. The team had discovered that some of the less tech-savvy individuals on their staff were undermining progress. They had built their own processes using offline spreadsheets, databases, unintegrated internet software, and other methods to get their jobs done. The team also found a few people who could not say no and took on more work than they could handle, creating dams and reservoirs in the process. Everything slowed down when orders got to those people.

For ABC's progress to be sustainable, Frank would have to make sure no one could go off-process like that again.

INVASIVE ECOSYSTEMS

Over the years, I have seen too many companies rise to new heights, just to suddenly lose all of their momentum and fall back to new lows. Too often, nobody had a clue why this happened. How could any company achieve so much, then totally stumble just as fast?

A number of years ago, I read a trade magazine article for the software industry. It mentioned that the CEO needed to take responsibility for the internal culture of the organization. The reason was because all it takes is one new individual joining the company for the culture to quickly erode.

The same is true of Your Opportunity River ecosystem. This ecosystem is the culture that allows your entire team to establish optimization of your river as the healthiest way to run your company. If just one individual, anywhere in your company, brings in another company's ecosystem, that ecosystem can act like an invasive species that could multiply and spread throughout the organization rapidly.

And all it takes is one new person, anywhere in your organization. Earlier in this book, I spoke about a bend resulting from a combination of a small disturbance and time. That disturbance could be a new machine operator on the shop floor, a new CFO, a new buyer, a new salesperson—anyone who works with a different set of rules and brings a different ecosystem into your company.

Such risks are particularly high when there's a change in leadership. A number of years ago, I worked with a company whose owner was set to retire and pass the torch to his son. The owner was aggressive, meticulous, and understood the ecosystem of his company. He had excellent RPT in place, enough that his company had quadrupled revenue over a few short years, with the goal to double it again. The key to this success was the owner's focus on daily metrics.

If one of the metrics suffered, he would determine what went wrong and how to correct it. Whether the obstacle he discovered involved a vendor, the quality of the material, machine setup, or a back office task, he was on it. As a result of his focus, their shop floor ran like a fast-flowing, highly profitable Opportunity River.

Once the owner stepped away, though, the ecosystem quickly changed. The new president did not follow the internal controls of his father. He abandoned the metrics his father utilized daily. That's all it took to break the internal processes and create new obstacles in the river. Within a year, the company was floundering. Instead of doubling revenue again, the company was just trying to stay afloat. It missed delivery dates, lost customers, lost employees, and lost money—all by taking an eye off the ecosystem.

The reason behind this is simple. Your Opportunity River ecosystem represents all the process improvements, all the resource optimization, and the right mix of technology to raise the riverbanks and allow your organization to hit new heights. Allowing any individual to change an ecosystem they do not fully understand or appreciate will plant an invasive practice that will rapidly infiltrate your river without you ever knowing what is happening. Without sufficient oversight, the change will inevitably disrupt the balance of that ecosystem and reduce your hard-earned efficiency and profitability. Left unattended, the changes in culture and process can spread to others in the organization and lead to catastrophic results.

MONITORING THE FLOW

Once Frank had ABC Fab's Opportunity River flowing rapidly, he feared the company would face the same issues as the one just cited. His solution started with making sure the entire team understood the new ecosystem.

Frank made a point of sharing the vision he had for the company. With better organization and fewer obstacles, everyone's job would be more straightforward, profits would be higher, and that would allow the company to offer more job security. There were a lot of reasons for everyone to buy into the Opportunity River ecosystem.

Once he had commitment across the organization, he could focus on installing metrics to make sure new obstacles weren't creeping into the process.

With a handful of daily, weekly, and monthly metrics, he could be sure the process continued to work without backsliding. Essentially, he created a series of flow monitors to measure the river's current using metrics. Those metrics allowed him to see the results of changes happening in his organization. With a watchful eye on leading indicators of every tributary, Frank and his team could monitor revenue and profit margin changes throughout the ecosystem, allowing them to respond quickly to issues when needed.

These metrics are valuable everywhere, but particular focus should be placed on the back office. By installing metrics across your back office, you can monitor a part of your ecosystem that is typically ignored. That doesn't mean Your Opportunity River should exclude the shop floor—because shop floor metrics can be a leading indicator of obstacles in the ecosystem—but since the back office is often where obstacles first appear, be sure to monitor it as well. Such metrics will make sure your ecosystem continues to properly leverage the strengths of your RPT. This constant monitoring will ensure your entire team, throughout the organization, maintains the new ecosystem and doesn't erode it.

Once the ecosystem is in place, with metrics to monitor the flow, you need to create the corporate infrastructure to minimize erosion. An Opportunity River ecosystem is built on process optimization and is part of a continuous improvement process. It is a journey and not a destination. The aim is to allow for change but only when it is mindfully and carefully considered.

Technology is changing all the time, and new methods of automation routinely hit the market. At the same time, an ecosystem in constant change is unstable and, as already mentioned, more likely to cause obstacles than remove them. Introducing new capabilities on a consistent basis will frustrate those people who just want to do their work and will create other obstructions through constant rounds of training. As every manufacturer knows, if you want to improve quality, reduce variability. A new manager may have a great idea for reorganizing the team, but if they're allowed to do that without careful forethought, it could lead to variability that creates obstructions elsewhere in the river.

Therefore, internal procedures should be managed by an ecosystem team, preferably one that includes managers. No one in the organization should be allowed to invoke change unilaterally—even new leadership. All changes must be brought forward to this team who determines the viability and only then, grants approval. This will keep some level of consistency and avoid hasty or thoughtless change, while still allowing you to evolve when those truly great new opportunities arise.

EVER-RENEWING SUCCESS

Your ability to deliver your products in any economy is at least as important as the products or services themselves. Your ability to deliver comes down to the Opportunity River ecosystem you put in place. The ecosystem in your business can be powerful, yet fragile; managed, yet permissive; and the source of your strength and resilience.

Through organization, clarity, management, and consistency, Your Opportunity River ecosystem can establish tributaries that deliver enduring expectations and lasting success. Monitoring metrics will maintain the straight, fast flow of the tributaries, while keeping your team open to positive evolution. In other words, when done right, the ecosystem can be flexible and durable enough to be truly evergreen.

As you chart your path to ever-renewing, ever-growing success, you can even label your evolving processes. Frank launched ABC Fab 2.0 after absorbing the lessons of the Opportunity River. But he wasn't done. Further improvement led to ABC Fab 3.0, and later, 4.0. Each new edition of the river instantly told everyone in the organization that improvements in the ecosystem were on their way. It rallied the entire team to get on board. It set the expectation for dramatic growth. And that growing, dynamic ecosystem is what allowed ABC Fab to dominate their industry to such a degree their competitors simply couldn't keep up. To allow team members who just wanted to do their daily tasks without interruption, the 2.0, 3.0, 4.0 process minimized variability until the next evolution came into place. The entire organization benefited, while it reduced the stresses of a constantly changing infrastructure.

SCAN HERE

Scan now for a quick video summary of this chapter!

Dive into key insights in seconds.

https://qrco.de/yor7uVD0

CHAPTER 8

CREATING FLOW MONITORS

TO ACHIEVE THAT DREAM OF ABC FAB 2.0, 3.0, 4.0, and beyond, Frank needed metrics to make sure his organization was running smoothly. Yet everywhere he looked, none of the key performance indicators (KPIs) measured back office efficiency. Most of the KPIs were shop floor metrics; whether the Top 10, or Top 20, or a litany of eighty-three manufacturing metrics, they didn't focus on measuring the flow of revenue through the back office. Searching through back office KPIs, he found metrics like customer satisfaction score, time to process invoices, revenue per employee, and even on-time delivery. Unfortunately, none of those metrics gave Frank what he wanted, because his intent for each metric was that it was simple to measure, requiring little to no manual effort to maintain. His team thought that revenue per employee would fit best, yet Frank said, "It is too broad. If you measure revenue per employee across the back office, how would it have identified the obstacles we found in scheduling, much less a new obstacle in customer service or even engineering? We need a better metric."

Frank and his team found that ABC Fab's new ERP system allowed them to track costs better and more accurately than ever before. Within a few months, the job costing and accounting people had timely and accurate labor, material, and outside costs, and with a couple months' more analysis, they would have their overhead cost allocations nailed down. This would give ABC Fab supreme confidence in their overall job costing, as well as their gross profits by product line tributaries. With those numbers in place, ABC Fab's CFO told Frank that he could create a financial statement supporting schedule from their ERP system that would show product line revenues and gross profits over any period they needed, even as detailed as monthly trends over many years.

Frank joked facetiously about how many spreadsheets and how much manual data entry it would take, recalling the inventory issues resulting from offline spreadsheets for scheduling jobs through the shop. To his surprise, the CFO said none. They would come directly from the ERP's financial system, along with monthly financial statements, requiring no manual data entry or extra effort. Still not convinced, Frank quipped about waiting for up to thirty days to get financial statements as needed in the past. The CFO said that was their old system. With the new ERP and far better controls, they had accurate financial information in three days following the end of the month.

This information had Frank's mind going into overdrive. To make sure he was hearing everything correctly, he wanted some clarification. He said, "So what you are saying is, we have better, more accurate job costing, including the detail of labor, materials, and outside costing, with improvements in overhead allocations?"

"Absolutely!"

Frank continued, "That means not only do we have accurate and timely product line tributary revenue and gross profits, but we also have more accurate bills-of-materials and shop floor routings, where those costs came from?"

Again, the response was, "Absolutely!"

Amazed, Frank said, "So we have continuous running revenue and gross profit information month by month, quarter by quarter, and year by year? Does that include charting product line tributary trends?"

The answer was an emphatic YES.

Frank and the team knew at that moment, they would be able to track trends to quickly see when profit levels started to erode, indicating flood stage or drought. This was something they'd never had in the history of ABC Fab. They had financial information from past years with the old ERP that gave them company-wide profit margins at the end of the year. They could use those records to guesstimate past flood stage levels. Frank felt that if the intended purpose of the strategies noted thus far in this book were working, they would use those new charts to see increased profitability percentages at greater revenue levels than ever before.

The CFO pulled Frank aside. He showed Frank that he had already put together a sample schedule showing that the strategies were working. They were already seeing higher revenues by month than ever before, with greater profits than they experienced at even lower revenue levels of the past. The CFO also told Frank that due to greater utilization on the shop floor resulting from back office improvements, they were currently over-allocating overhead, another indication the strategies were working, and once they got overhead allocations dialed in, costs would be lower and the results would be even better.

Frank mentioned that he had been watching on-time delivery performance improve over the last couple months, while inventory levels had trended down. That all made sense to him because the improved accuracies in the bills-of-materials and shop routings (the manufacturing processes needed to make any specific part or component) would also improve ABC Fab's scheduling, which was key to making better delivery promises and improved purchasing processes.

Frank and the team were fired up based on the results, yet Frank brought back his previous concern. He said, "This is excellent news, but what are we going to do to get some sort of metrics that help us measure our back office efficiency? Measuring revenue per employee is not going to give us the detail we need to find present and future obstacles."

Frank suggested they bring in their continuous improvement specialist. After explaining the issue, the specialist suggested being more granular than just revenue by total employees. She said, "Let's track revenue by employee at the department level." After a bit of discussion, they agreed. If they monitored the number of employees in departments, including sales, customer services, purchasing, scheduling, inventory, accounting, etc., and divided each number into revenue, it would result in a new metric indicating the amount of revenue each person a department is able to support. So if they had four people in purchasing and $50 million in revenue, each person could support $12.5 million in revenue. Frank liked these metrics because they would also show whether the strategy to harvest significant value from internal resources was working. If they tracked total employees by month, by department, they would be able to measure how much higher the banks of the river would increase, meaning operating the department at higher levels of revenue per employee than before, without hitting flood stage.

Frank asked how they could pull this off. Once again, the answer was their new ERP accounting system. It had something called "statistical accounts" in the chart-of-accounts. The CFO said they could use departmental statistical accounts to show the number of employees by department.

Since they were already tracking revenue, it would be an easy equation to divide revenue by department employee count. They joked about needing another spreadsheet until the CFO mentioned the accounting system could easily provide this information, just like it could provide the tributary revenue and gross profit information.

That is what the group needed to hear. They could now measure each department's ability to support the revenue of the company. So in the example of each purchasing department employee supporting $12.5 million in revenue, they could measure whether revenue could grow $25 million with no need for additional purchasing staff, much less the two people required based on the current metric. This would also show how well the RPT formula worked to leverage automation to speed up internal processes, while minimizing employee effort to harvest significant value from their current people resources. And if they were able to have an accurate production schedule, they could see how the company would also benefit from improved delivery performance with lower inventory levels, less cash tied up in inventory, less warehouse space needed, and with less material handling.

Frank could see by the light in their eyes that the team was excited. The CFO mentioned that the inventory levels were going down, which was already resulting in an increase in cash. Frank said that he noticed less inventory with less need for pallet racking. He mentioned, if this keeps going, they will have the option to put more production machines in areas that used to hold inventory, if ever needed, thereby leveraging their existing facilities without needing more, and at the same time, converting space that contributed to higher overhead into productive space that would increase revenue.

Before they got too far, there were guardrails that had to be put up. They all agreed that measuring revenue by employee by department could not go down to the product line tributary level, because nearly all departments worked across all product line tributaries at any company location. Yet measuring by location would also provide them visibility by department to see if the numbers were slipping, like when a new employee from XYZ Fab brought along their processes into ABC Fab. It would also indicate which department and at what revenue level new obstacles were developing.

The discussion went to the what-if stage, specifically what if one of the department flood stage flow meters went south, or if a product line tributary flow meter found a new flood stage. The answer was the new flow meters would help triangulate what department(s) were impacted by the revenue level, along with what the new flood stage revenue level was for that department. That would allow for faster triage of the problem and whether the problem was due to the lack of conformance to the internal operating procedures or whether it was a change to the RPT combination for that specific department. The flow meter would indicate whether a new obstacle existed in a department, such as someone switching from the ERP system to offline spreadsheets, or whether the company was outgrowing their ERP system, or even where the new level of revenue exposed a problem of too many manual tasks in the specific department.

Everyone agreed that if an obstacle was found, they could use their Business Intelligence (BI) application to find out if the obstacle happened because of a change in the revenue mix from the relevant product line tributaries or just overall growth revenue. They also found out that their BI system could easily look at bookings (the analysis of outstanding unshipped orders) by product line tributary to determine whether obstacles might see further challenges based on orders coming downstream.

What the team at ABC Fab became increasingly aware of was the incredible interdependence within their back office operations. More importantly, how the lever-moving benefits of highly integrated ERP technology could be used to optimize the resource, process, and technology pumps to speed revenue through the organization while creating significant whitespace to grow revenues and profits before spending an additional dime on any of those resources.

WHEN IS TECHNOLOGY THE SOLUTION?

With all the technology on the market, you would think it should provide the solution. Perhaps it's a bit surprising to you it's taken so long to focus on technology. To start this book, I focused on mapping Your Opportunity River and determining the obstacles. Why map it? Why not just get to the technology that can solve all your problems?

The key to answering those questions lies in what I have experienced in my years in manufacturing, business, and life in general. There is an excess of what is commonly called "mutual mystification" in this world. That, simply put, involves people having a different understanding about a topic from what was intended—some diametrically opposed to the intended thought. Often, we fail to recognize this possibility in our own communication. How many of us walk away from a conversation assuming what was heard was understood precisely the same by everyone involved?

This misunderstanding is the source of many of the obstacles in your organization. And you have to address this issue before technology can be any help. To help solve this, I introduced Your Opportunity River map. A significant percentage of people are visually oriented, meaning they need to see concepts visually to understand them.

A visual, such as a map, is a better tool for synchronizing people to a common and consistent thought. This becomes more important when the map is broken down into departments, illustrating the obstacles and where they exist. At this point, technology isn't important to the process. The reason is those who start the process of drawing Your Opportunity River and labeling obstructions might not be technology savvy. Why force technology into the process of visualizing the obstacles that are keeping a company from being more successful? Writing down the revenue and gross profit margins for each tributary could be done on a spreadsheet or on a statement from your general ledger system, but as with the map, you will lose those who do not know how to read a financial statement supporting schedule. We are really looking at the best method to align as many people as possible on your team in the easiest way possible.

At this point, technology is not a key consideration because the key should be to understand the process of finding obstacles in your resources, processes, and technology. The main aim of this book is to help you get very, very good at understanding obstacles and differentiating them from business as usual. RPT will continue to change, yet the real skill in this journey is finding the obstacles associated with any of them.

Most of Frank's gains came from this central insight. It was only *after* that was absorbed that technology became his ally. Otherwise, technology might be the problem. Only afterward can it be a component of the solution that can open up revenue and profit floodgates for your organization. Without the clarity of Your Opportunity River, technology can be as confusing as the rest of your processes. Leveraging technology to solve specific challenges is far better than using tech for the sake of tech.

Technology becomes a problem when multiple technologies are cobbled together to provide an intended solution. Trust me on this, trying to integrate disparate technologies rarely creates an enriching solution, yet a lot of money is spent to achieve the goal. Think of tying two technologies like an ERP system and a spreadsheet together as an example. If you must manually export, manipulate, and import data over and over again to leverage the capabilities of each, it is not an enriching solution. Why? Because exporting and manipulating data consumes whitespace, rather than creating it. Does it make any difference if you are using an ETL (extract, translate, and load) tool to move the data? The surprising answer is no! Most people don't realize how much time and effort goes into developing their own tools. They all consume whitespace. Those tools should already exist for you to deploy solutions, not to develop them.

Creating whitespace is the ultimate goal of Your Opportunity River. You want to put in place the lowest cost method of raising the banks of your river to profitably scale your revenue, while at the same time leveraging whitespace to keep your overhead low to weather industry droughts. This allows you to harvest significant value from your internal resources before investing another dime, and does it without increasing cost.

Harvesting maximum whitespace is where ERP systems will either make or break the process for any organization. But once you understand that an ERP's purpose should be to create whitespace, it becomes easier to understand how that technology can let your organization down. For instance, as mentioned with the toggling tax whirlpool described in Chapter 3, toggling between screens and processes is an example of where ERP systems *consume* tremendous amounts of whitespace as opposed to creating it.

Another example of whitespace consumption is the illusion of application simplicity. Many applications that impress people by looking very simple are not good at optimizing organizational interdependence. In other words, they look easy, but many manual workarounds are needed to make up for the lack of broad and deep integration. Those workarounds contribute to systemic bends, dams, reservoirs, and whirlpools that consume whitespace, taxing your company's ability to maximize revenue and profits.

The good news is all the ERP capabilities we see Frank use in this book are available to you right now. I know that because I sell an ERP solution, including a suite of internally developed applications that can do everything I've claimed, such as generating maximum whitespace for manufacturing organizations in our supported industries. So yes, technology can be and is the right solution for the straightest, fastest, most effective flow of Your Opportunity River. And it should be the essential catalyst for growing your organization to uniquely satisfy your customers' needs.

But it can only do that if you have all the nontechnological insights in this book already in place. It's the additional piece that can really open opportunities for your company to excel—but only if you understand when and how to create maximum whitespace as compared to when and where it is wreaking havoc on the resources in your company.

**Scan now for a quick video
summary of this chapter!**

Dive into key insights in seconds.

https://qrco.de/yor8uVD1

CHAPTER 9

RIVER OF DREAMS

AT THIS POINT IN THE PROCESS, YOU HAVE COVERED everything needed to take your manufacturing organization to another level. You have Your Opportunity River map for everyone in the company to clearly understand the tributaries of your organization, including how they generate revenue and profit margins for your company. Going forward, the practice of updating these numbers on a monthly basis will create a baseline to measure future progress. You've also charted obstacles that disrupted Your Opportunity River and straightened them to improve the speed and shorten the flow of the impacted tributaries. By evaluating the product line revenue and profit margin data, you will see margins improve, especially in revenue ranges that were once decimated with flood stage.

By optimizing the mix of your RPT at every step of your

internal operations, you will optimize internal operations and open the floodgates to even greater revenues.

Once done, it is time to let the revenue race through Your Opportunity River, leveraging greater efficiencies and harvesting far greater profits. The results will show up in the revenue and profit margin metrics you continue to monitor. These will be the key indicators that Your Opportunity River ecosystem of optimized RPT is consistently being followed. The goal is to find your organization's revenue and profitability upper limits before investing another dime on internal resources (people, inventory, machinery, or facilities).

As the profits flow smoothly and quickly through your river, you may wake up one day to discover you are in charge of a mighty Mississippi of your own. But why stop there?

While this is happening, you may find what once seemed impossible increasingly becomes viable. The many dreams of business growth that were limited due to pushback from lenders and eroded profits naturally resurface. With the effort of just trying to keep your river flowing gone, you may discover an opportunity to transform your business not just into the Mississippi but into the Amazon of your world.

THE AMAZON OPPORTUNITY RIVER IS BORN

In 1994, a young Jeff Bezos, impressed by the rapid growth of the internet, wrote up the business plan for what he eventually called Amazon. Bezos selected the name while scanning a dictionary. He was struck by the river's size—it's the largest drainage basin of any river in the world. It was the perfect name for a company he intended to make the world's biggest everything store.

But Bezos didn't start selling everything. He knew that was unfeasible. So, he narrowed his Amazon River vision down to a single tributary, books. He aimed to dominate that market by offering a vastly larger selection than even the most well-stocked brick-and-mortar retailers. Eventually, as the company grew, Amazon expanded to more tributaries, including CDs, DVDs, software, electronics, and ultimately to everything we know Amazon to be today, which is expanding as you are reading.

Bezos's ambitions were written into the Amazon logo itself. The very simple design, with the smile under the name, is also an arrow pointing from the letter A to the letter Z. But Bezos could only achieve that by growing his river one tributary at a time, expanding from one product to another, until Amazon dominated the entire e-commerce world, offering everything from A to Z.

ADDING TRIBUTARIES

The Amazon River, like Amazon the company, is a vast complex of tributaries joining the main river. With far more tributaries than the Mississippi River, it is by far the bigger, more powerful river system.

Mother Nature is never wrong. The concept of using multiple tributaries to form into a larger river basin yields far more benefits than growing your river on the back of a single product. By growing through tributaries, your growth is systematic and scalable, offering more of what your customers want and creating additional challenges for competitors to overtake you.

Many think Amazon the company is no more than its products, but actually it's the ecosystem that is their secret weapon. Once the ecosystem of optimized RPT Bezos developed for selling books was perfected, it became ever easier to expand into other similar offerings and immediately dominate the field each time. If you can sell books online, it doesn't take much effort to sell CDs. If you can sell CDs, you can sell DVDs. If you have designed your ecosystem to leverage the scalability of technology, it will free up the resources you have and automate your processes, unlocking rapid growth that is entirely organic and highly profitable.

In this respect, growing your business requires more than just constant review of Your Opportunity River map. It requires a keen eye looking for ways to shore up existing tributaries to handle hypergrowth, as well as adding new tributaries that complement your existing offerings. What complementary products can you offer to those you already make? What services can you provide? Can you offer field service, depot repairs, maintenance contracts on your products, stocking programs for customers, or quick ship products? Are there accessories you can resell from distributors without stocking? Are there suppliers you currently buy from or outsource to who you could acquire to get top priority, lower costs, and quicker deliveries?

A THOUSAND DREAMS

It's been said, "A person with their health has a thousand dreams; a person without it has only one." The same is true of opportunity. A highly profitable company is the source of a thousand dreams; a company with low profits has only one. The question now is how far you take those dreams and how quickly you achieve them.

The ABC Fab team had their ecosystem of RPT in place, with their revenue streams flowing faster and straighter than ever before. Their monthly monitoring of every tributary's revenue and profitability gave the team proof that profit margins were increasing at faster rates than in the past, even as they realized record revenues. This gave them the comfort their ecosystem optimization had increased the height of the riverbanks, so they could reap greater revenues without hitting flood stage as they did in the past. The profitability, growth, and straighter tributaries allowed ABC Fab to invest in Electronic Data Interchange (EDI) software to electronically enter the majority of customer orders, vastly reducing the human effort to manually enter customer orders. The river started flowing even more rapidly. Everything in the organization was electronic, even out on the shop floor. No paper anywhere, so changes could be caught at a moment's notice, even in the shop.

For the first time in what seemed like forever, the ABC Fab team was so relaxed. They had more orders than ever before, yet nobody was stressed this time around. The team members got into their weekly meeting with no fires to put out or angry customers calling on the status of their orders. In fact, their customers now had confidence in the delivery dates that were provided by ABC Fab's customer service team. Customers were moving to ABC Fab and away from their competition. The ecosystem was working so well that they started dreaming about the future. They talked about buying more machines, building bigger facilities, and finding more customers. While Frank acknowledged those options, he had a bigger vision. Frank brought out his ABC Fab Opportunity River map and this time viewed it like Bezos viewed the Amazon River. Frank saw the map as ABC's foundation to expand in any way they could imagine.

Recognizing this, he pushed for a bolder vision: "Let's find more customers—but let's do it smartly. We already service the majority of customers within five hundred miles of our facilities. Finding more customers will force us to look farther away, and that will increase our freight costs, negatively impacting our prices. After all, every security enclosure is fully assembled and shipped on a truck. Inside the enclosure, there is a lot of open space. When we assemble the enclosures in our shop, we tie up precious space for weeks until the product is ready to ship. So, what if we changed our home facility to manufacture enclosure panels? We could create panel assembly lines and build them faster than ever before. We could put panels for multiple enclosures on a truck at the same time, lowering our freight costs."

The rest of the team seemed lost. Frank was talking about panels. What about the enclosures?

That's when an engineer jumped in. "I get it. We find and acquire metal fab companies in hub areas of our targeted customer base. We can ship multiple panels to those facilities, and they can assemble enclosures and ship them direct to the customer."

He continued, "What if we stopped thinking about our enclosures as one-off custom fabrications? What if we made panel sections that were interchangeable? We could make our enclosures a simpler process of assembling the pieces together, while reducing variability, increasing speed, and improving quality."

Frank slapped the table with excitement. "Exactly! We are constrained today on our assembly space. If we built panels in that space, we could feed at least four different facilities with panels, which would expand our velocity, opening up our market to customers that are beyond our reach today.

"Until we get up to speed, we could use the same trucks to expand the market for our fabricated assemblies. This will generate far more profits, creating the ability to invest in robotics right here at home to automate our panel fabrication. That will allow our workforce to transition into our other product tributaries."

As Frank realized, this was one of many paths open to anyone who uses the Opportunity River. Suddenly, it becomes clear where to invest the influx of cash that your company starts earning after obstacles are cleared. If you wish to dominate your marketplace, this is how you expand your river, creating new tributaries and additional revenue sources—scaling your ecosystem across your industry.

THE SUCCESS TRAP

Your current river system is the sum total of everything you offer and your core expertise. As your river grows, you want to expand with convergent streams that flow naturally into your river and tributaries. Examine your main product or service offering as Bezos and Frank did. Your goal should be to offer other products, services, capabilities, and methods of serving your marketplace that align with that offering.

At the same time, avoid investing in divergent streams that do not flow naturally into Your Opportunity River. The failures of companies who have made this mistake are numerous. One of the inspirations of writing this book was observing companies who wasted years and enormous sums of money on tributaries they knew nothing about. In the words of Greg McKeown, author of *Essentialism*, they fell into the success trap that "leads to the undisciplined pursuit of more." Success, with a lack of discipline, results in companies launching unrelated products, buying unrelated businesses, and taking on risks way outside their core competency. Success can become a catalyst for failure, as the divergent stream consumes mind share that you should be devoting on your expertise.

Operating in a completely different river is a sport only megacompanies should be messing with—and even they should be very careful. There are so many examples of big companies making messy acquisitions way outside the realm of their expertise, such as when Rupert Murdoch's News Corp bought Myspace, AT&T bought NCR, Cisco bought Pure Digital, or Pepsi bought Yum! Brands. All of those ended badly. When you feel like you and your company foolishly invested in a new tributary, google one of these fiascos, and it should provide you with the consolation that even global players are capable of committing colossal blunders.

How do you avoid these mistakes? Focus first on your customers. As has been said countless times before, it is far easier to sell to an existing customer than to acquire a new one. Similarly, happy customers are your best brand representatives to gain new prospects. So a great strategy for business growth is to focus on creating more products and services to offer your existing customers. Serve your customers better, and they'll buy more from you, recommend you more often, and fuel your expansion into new areas.

GROWING THROUGH AUTOMATION

This is only possible, though, if your technology can scale with you. One of the key insights Bezos had about his business was the need to focus on making his business processes as streamlined as possible so they could be automated and run full-speed 24/7. Doing so took the drudgery off his people, allowing them to do more high value-added functions, making Amazon more scalable.

Let's consider an example. How profitable would Amazon be if they had order entry people dealing with every nuance of dealing with customers? Think about how many times people go on Amazon's website and put merchandise into a shopping cart, yet never purchase anything. Where would Amazon be if it hadn't used shopping cart automation to free up its people?

Similarly, how many times in your own business do you create a quote for a company that you never hear from again? What is the cost of that in your organization, especially if it happens in 80 to 92 percent of the estimates? What if that could be automated so the customer could "configure" their own product, even if they leave it in their shopping cart, freeing up your people in the process and reducing cost? What if it could simultaneously send an email to your sales team so they could follow up with the prospect to help close the deal? You could arm your sales team with precisely what the prospect wanted to buy. More importantly, the salesperson could see a 2-D or 3-D drawing, including dimensions, complete with your selling price, costs, and profit in advance. This potential is there for you.

Peter Diamandis, visionary, futurist, founder of Abundance 360 and X-Prize, and author of *The Future Is Better Than You Think*, says, "There are ways to take nearly anything from 'scarcity' to 'abundance' given the right tools." Ask yourself, what tools in this world are abundant that could help reduce the strain on other resources in your company and scale Your Opportunity River in the process? The answer is to leverage the abundance of technology to scale your most precious asset, your people, and design that into your eco-system. The proper use of technology for the right purpose is the secret weapon your business can use to outperform all of your competition.

Continue to focus on making your back office scalable and a vital component of your RPT ecosystem that powers your ability to build more products better, faster, and with higher quality than ever before. For manufacturers, their ecosys-tem needs to be exponentially scalable. The great thing about building the right ecosystem in the back office is the competition will never know how or why your company keeps winning. Dan Sullivan, founder of Strategic Coach and a mentor of mine, says, "The competition can easily see your front-office products through marketing and sales material, but they will never figure out your back office." Combining ecosystem resource optimization with strategic tributary growth, you could soon find your company being the Amazon of your industry. And you could soon be seeing those thousand dreams come true.

Scan now for a quick video summary of this chapter!

Dive into key insights in seconds.

https://qrco.de/yor9uVD2

SCAN HERE

CHAPTER 10

TWO VIEWS OF YOUR OPPORTUNITY RIVER

FRANK HAS USED HIS OPPORTUNITY RIVER MAP TO rethink the way ABC Fab does business. In the beginning, his map had just three main tributaries and two feeder tributaries. Now, with five locations, it has five major tributaries, each with their own product line feeder tributaries. In the beginning, the world of ABC Fab was a five-hundred-mile radius around their Midwest facility. Today, Frank's Opportunity River map overlays on a map of the United States, with tributaries from each of the satellite locations to the company headquarters. It extends two thousand miles from east to west and 1,400 miles from north to south. ABC Fab has become the juggernaut of their industry and has launched new products in additional industries. Frank has leveraged the RPT ecosystem throughout the entire organization, while maintaining focus on the company's strength as a metal fabricator.

Frank still tracks product line revenues and profit margins monthly for each location, including the location's net profit margins. Those tributaries are reviewed with monthly flow meters to make sure the metrics continue to create whitespace below the tops of riverbanks, maintaining space for ABC Fab to continue to grow profitably.

Additionally, his map has circles around each location, indicating the extent of each location's market space, which defines the size of his Opportunity River basin. It is within that geographical space that ABC Fab is the dominating force in the industry, with successful locations that are crucial to the communities, local economies, and the families of each person employed by ABC Fab. Frank sees the strength of the company as the combined strength of the entire team. Frank leverages the creativity and street smarts of his team by ensuring they all understand the concepts of their Opportunity River. Frank provides them the tools and support to make suggestions that continue to improve the operations of the company, as well as making product suggestions to maximize the ABC Fab Opportunity River Basin.

While amazed at how well his team has designed their Opportunity River map to grow the company systematically, Frank also views the map from the view of ABC's customers. By providing a one-stop solution to those customers in the geography of the river basin, he makes sure everyone at ABC Fab gives their current and prospective customers no reason to buy what they offer from anyone else. They have become the Amazon of their expanding world.

THE VIEW LOOKING DOWNRIVER

At this stage, I want you to look downstream, keeping your focus on the best way to grow your river basin by harvesting profits and putting some of them back into the business. You can do this by adding new products, new services, new acquisitions, new markets, and so on. The goal here is to make the mouth of your river, where it flows into the ocean (marketplace) as wide as possible to attract more and more customers.

As you look downstream, the view of the breadth of the river resulting from your tributaries should be a vast waterway that ideally flows into a "blue ocean," a term I first learned in W. Chan Kim's and Renée Mauborgne's book *Blue Ocean Strategy*. A blue ocean is an uncontested market space that you control because you reinvented your industry. Compare being in a blue ocean having little to no competition, with a red ocean where products have become a low-margin commodity and a vast pool of competitors eat each other alive by constantly lowering their prices.

Existing entirely in either type of ocean may sound overly simplistic, but this is your ultimate aim. If this process seems difficult, you can take solace from the fact that you will not be the first one to create new opportunities in otherwise commoditized industries.

One of our clients had twelve locations when we started with them. They were stalled at those twelve facilities. Once they improved their Opportunity River, they were able to create a more standardized organizational ecosystem and use that increased efficiency to quickly generate tremendous amounts of cash. They used that cash to capture the market by acquiring every competing location in a multistate region. Their count grew to thirty-three locations, which resulted in creating a blue ocean across their regional marketplace.

This is a journey companies have taken across many different industries, and it's a journey you can take too.

OFFER MORE AND DO MORE WITH WHAT YOU'VE GOT

Remember the old days when gas stations only sold gas, tires, and oil, along with soda and candy bars from vending machines? For years and years, change was minimal, and everyone suffered low profitability. The whole industry was a red ocean. Competition creates commoditization, which lowers prices and lowers margins. The only way out of this is to be the gas station that sells more than anyone else offers.

Enter QuikTrip, who finally figured out how to add the right tributaries and use that to dominate the competition.

QuikTrip created a gas station that still sold the standard items for your car but also offered car washes, groceries, hot food, drinks, over-the-counter drugs, cosmetics, and more.

QuikTrip's realization changed the market. Suddenly, gas stations realized that they could create their own space in the ocean by offering more pumps, putting in better lighting, providing a canopy to protect drivers from the weather, adding indoor, clean bathrooms, and offering far more options in their stores.

That is the kind of experience customers want, and it makes a difference. And if gas stations can improve, anyone can improve and grow using this same strategy, regardless of your industry or if you have a B2B or B2C business.

The downstream view isn't just about expanding what you offer, though. It's also doing more with what you already offer. We can see this clearly in the evolution of the livestock industry.

In the past, livestock were harvested solely for their meat. Today, the best of the best have found revenue opportunities for the entire carcass. When there was waste, there were costs associated with dealing with that waste, which drove profits down. Today, companies earn money for 100 percent of the animal and have lower costs.

KEEP GROWING

If companies can find growth in these highly commoditized industries, you should have more than enough hope to find opportunities in your business. In fact, you should look at Your Opportunity River with optimism. After all, your manufacturing business has Your Opportunity River map, which provides far more clarity on operations than most businesses have. And that clarity provides more opportunity for new ideas on how to expand, differentiate, and leverage your core competencies as you add more tributaries.

Now that your company's operations are clear to everyone, those ideas could come from anywhere in the business. Different individuals have unique backgrounds and experiences. Those unique perspectives can become instrumental in developing growth ideas.

To harness your full potential, be open to any kind of opportunity—as long as it strengthens Your Opportunity River. A new tributary of providing repair or replacement parts for your equipment could be a differentiator in your industry. The nature of this tributary could be very different depending on your customers' needs. It could be a revenue stream of preventive maintenance, depot repair, or in-the-field repair services for your products. Maybe you do not have a large service organization, are understaffed, or do not have people in the field who know your products well. You might acquire other companies that are in the field to provide such services or initiate maintenance agreements with the customer and pay field reps to perform necessary services. My company has clients who even service their competitor's products. Their rationale is to perform a better service than their competitors, make a profit while doing so, and build a relationship with a customer that may pay off next time the customer needs more products or services.

There is similar potential for each tributary. Every tributary brings more unique offerings to the table that all fit a core competency of the organization. As the river grows, so do products and services, sales, customers, profits, competitive advantage, and company value. Anyone can see how the small creek at the beginning of the Mississippi River has far fewer opportunities than it has as it moves farther south, growing and growing. A small creek can only float an inner tube. Farther downstream, it supports locks and electricity-producing dams, tremendous amounts of commerce from barges, paddlewheel boats that have gambling and river cruises, yacht clubs, restaurants, cities, and more.

The ongoing search for new ways to create and support customers should be topics of continuous discussions inside the organization. Too many businesses keep their heads down, doing what they do, with little time invested in creating new streams of revenue.

If you want your company to grow, you have to look beyond what you already do. Following this path also leads to becoming part of a company that already has a blue ocean. Major companies are not easily duplicated. Often, the best option is to be acquired. When the companies are cash-producing machines with solid systems, solid marketing, and solid profits, they create the opportunities to be acquired—and at very high multiples.

Any smart company looking to make an acquisition will see the opportunity to buy at lower multiples when the business is poorly automated, very inefficient, and has poor cash flow and significant debt. They see the opportunity to turn the company around, and in some cases, sell it at a premium. The benefits of high multiples go to those who have higher than normal margins, solid cash flow, and strong systems that support scalable growth. Do your research and grow your company; the payback is there when you do it right.

THE VIEW LOOKING UPRIVER

This is the fun part of Your Opportunity River. You now understand the view looking downstream, observing it from the viewpoint of how you've grown your company, your marketplace, your revenue, and your profits. Now turn Your Opportunity River map and look upriver, taking a hard look at your business to see it through the eyes of your customer.

Always keep in mind that your customer wants to know, "What's in it for me?" They are looking upriver to see what you have available for them. They really don't care what you are doing for yourself. Give the customer many great reasons for seeing Your Opportunity River as their Opportunity River that satisfies their needs, and your business will grow and thrive.

When your customer is looking at your business, what do they see? Luckily, they should see that you should have a lot to offer. If you have scaled your business with high efficiency where all of the tributaries have converged at various places across the river basin, you should be amassing a massive Opportunity River, with strong product offerings, the fastest deliveries, excellent margins, and every other competitor competing for low-margin business. You should be getting customers large and small because you have a product/service offering that fits your ideal customer demographics.

They should not see a hodgepodge of unrelated products or vastly different marketplaces. Rather, they should see a collection of products that show your expertise and your commitment to their businesses. More importantly, your customers and prospects should see a partner they want to do business with—because you fit their needs better than anyone else, offering complementary products and services that lead to their own convenience and opportunities. Your sales and marketing people should easily and consistently be able to sell your customers everything you have to support them. Each customer should see your company as being highly integrated, totally unique, and the perfect fit for their business or family.

You have to continually improve your river by looking at it through your customers' eyes. Are you satisfying all of the requirements and needs of your customers? Can you offer a quick ship program? Can you leverage software that helps your customers configure their own unique products while providing them rapid price quotes? Can you offer a repair program that keeps your products running? Can you assist your customers with a higher level of fulfillment and distribution? Can you send an A-Team of your people to your customers' sites to help them design their product? Can your team show them how to better utilize your products? Can you move production closer to a big customer to help reduce shipping costs and create closer relationships? It may require a head scratch and some thinking outside of the box, but in the end, not only do you win but your customers win.

This process will generate new customers and retain existing customers so both become customers for life. Those customers who have already engaged in business with you will see new complementary offerings that will endear them to your business in ways they did not have in the past. When the customer only sees your company as a small river, then opportunities will be limited for you and for them. They have little loyalty, giving work based on shopping for the lowest price, while destroying your profits as a result. Once you have more to offer, they have more reason to stay with you.

Even if you do have a narrow product offering and stick close to it, look for ways you can expand your niche. Are there ways to use those capabilities to offer products faster, with fewer delays, where you make a delivery promise and keep that promise?

There is no rule in business that says you can't stick to a

single niche. However, be forewarned: a narrow river means a greater risk that a competitor will come along with more products, more services, and more solutions, and they will have the ability to make the same product you do, only cheaper and with equal quality. For this reason, it's far better to expand Your Opportunity River with considerable offerings and very little reason for anybody in your world to look elsewhere. Such a focus will allow you to dominate those who stick to a single narrow niche. In strong economies, you will own a far larger share of the market, and in times of drought, you will have more retained profits and wider market specialization to weather the storm.

As you make further improvements, adjust your marketing to speak to all you're offering them. Let them know you are catering to their needs and doing so in a way that is very convenient for them.

YOUR FUTURE POTENTIAL

Amazon (the company) can be considered a river with many tributaries—many offerings. It has grown powerful in its size and capability to service its customers in seemingly limitless ways. It never stops flowing. Its constant forward momentum and abundant supply of customers and prospects make it a juggernaut. The goal is for you to design Your Opportunity River to grow and be a force to be reckoned with.

Create Your Opportunity River as one that looks beautifully crafted and meticulously maintained—a river that impresses everyone, including the toughest critics. When you have reached that destination, you get to choose the customers and markets you work with.

It is time to start designing and creating the future of Your Opportunity River. If you follow the ideas in this book, the opportunities will be endless. All it takes is a bit of imagination, a bit of infrastructure, and the dedication to follow through. If you do that, anything will be possible.

Scan now for a quick video summary of this chapter!

Dive into key insights in seconds.

https://qrco.de/yorAuVD3

SCAN HERE

CONCLUSION

I HAVE A LIFELONG LOVE OF MANUFACTURING, AND it has been hard watching so many incredible businesses struggle for so long. Day after day, year after year, decade after decade, they fight against the current, always hoping just to keep their heads above the water.

That was the reason I developed Your Opportunity River. I am confident that this system will allow you to not just keep your manufacturing company afloat but to ride the waves of improvements to previously unimagined success.

Along the way, I would love to be a partner in helping you with your success. In my business, called The Lake Companies, our team has developed software for the manufacturing industry with the goal to forever change how the manufacturing world leverages technology to run their businesses more successfully.

Having this vision for such a long time has offered us the ability to see our marketplace from a different perspective. This view has allowed us to design software and make strategic technology decisions that offer hundreds and thousands of daily whitespace-generating benefits for our customers. Those benefits are so well hidden in their back office operations that their competitors and ours cannot begin to see them.

It is my wish that you find greatness in these methods, and they lead you, your company, and your fellow team members to the best of success in your business for many years to come.

ACKNOWLEDGMENTS

THE PROCESS OF WRITING A BOOK HAS BEEN LONGER and harder than I ever imagined. While it has taken some time, it has also resulted in a better product. Although the mom I lost when I was nine years old is not physically here, she has listened to my nightly prayers and been at my side for the entire journey. Mom, my faith in you is everlasting, and I am eternally grateful for your support.

The germ of this book came from Dan Sullivan, CEO of Strategic Coach. Who knew that a stream metaphor, with varying current breaks in the stream, delivered about fourteen years ago, could become Your Opportunity River. I took the concept in a totally different direction, yet I am deeply grateful to Dan and Strategic Coach for planting the seed and the support I have received from my fellow coach members.

I also want to recognize Joe Polish and his Genius Network program. Joe, you don't know how much inspiration you have provided, as well as the many GN members who have offered advice, ideas, and direction on how to get this book started and finished. The combined support has been invaluable.

Thank you, Summer Mulder, CEO of The Draw Shop, for the gentle nudging to keep the process going and for the illustration ideas used in this book. It has brought life and additional clarity to Your Opportunity River.

A process that takes years can have its ups and downs, yet my wife, Debbie, along with our team at The Lake Companies, most notably Stacy, have heard these thoughts and ideas so many times, they could have probably written this book themselves. Thank you for your patience and encouragement along the way.